Safeguarding and Protecting Children:
a guide for sportspeople

sports coach UK is the brand name of The National Coaching Foundation
and has been such since April 2001

ISBN: 978-1-905540-26-6

First and second editions
Developed from an original text by Maureen Crouch (NSPCC) in conjunction with the
Royal Yachting Association (RYA) and edited by Penny Crisfield (NCF).

Third edition
Author: Gil Lester
The publishers would like to thank the following for their valuable input to this handbook:
Steve Boocock, Tim Gardner, Andy Rangecroft, Biddy Rowe and Hamish Telfer.

Fourth edition
Revised by: Nick Slinn
Grateful thanks to: Vicky Bailey, Carole Billington-Wood, Simon Jones, Kathleen McInulty, Steve McQuaid,
Heather Moir, Iain Moir, Paul Stephenson, Anne Tiivas, Steve Woolland and Matthew Williams.

Cover photo: Alan Edwards

Published on behalf of
sports coach UK by

sports coach UK
114 Cardigan Road
Headingley
Leeds LS6 3BJ
Tel: 0113-274 4802 Fax: 0113-275 5019
Email: coaching@sportscoachuk.org
Website: www.sportscoachuk.org

Patron: HRH The Princess Royal

Coachwise Ltd
Chelsea Close
Off Amberley Road
Armley
Leeds LS12 4HP
Tel: 0113-231 1310
Fax: 0113-231 9606
Email: enquiries@coachwise.ltd.uk
Website: www.coachwise.ltd.uk

sports coach UK will ensure that it has professional and ethical values and that all
its practices are inclusive and equitable.

90657:13

In 2006, Government figures indicated that over 30,000[1] children in the UK were officially registered as being in need of protection from abuse. Research indicates that abuse is significantly under-reported and under-registered, and the unofficial estimate of children in need of protection is many thousands more. Children may be abused regardless of their age, race, gender, culture, religious belief, disability or sexual identity. They are usually abused by people they know and trust – these could be people from inside or outside the family, adults or other young people. Although there are, as yet, no official statistics for the incidence of abuse in sport, the vast majority of sports organisations are dealing with cases of poor practice and abuse arising inside and outside their sport's environment. The fact that there are growing numbers of reported cases of abuse in sport is evidence enough to justify that every possible measure must be taken to ensure that sport offers a safe experience for children.

People who work with children in sport on a regular basis may be able to provide an important link in identifying a child who has been, or is, at risk of being harmed. Therefore, all those directly or indirectly involved with children's sport have a responsibility to:

- review their own practice in sport situations to ensure that it complies with advocated and recognised codes of conduct

- identify their values and feelings in relation to child abuse and recognise how they might potentially impact on their responses

- be able to recognise signs and indicators of child abuse and understand the impact of abuse on children

- respond in an appropriate way to children who disclose that they are being abused

- take appropriate action if concerns are raised that suggest a child is being abused.

A number of enquiry reports into the deaths of children in the UK (eg Kennedy McFarlane in Scotland and, more recently, Victoria Climbie in England) have highlighted shortcomings in the way a wide range of agencies and services worked together to protect vulnerable children. The impact of the lessons learned from these tragedies has been felt across the UK. In response, national strategies have been developed to ensure that children's needs are met both by organisations and individuals who work for them. These strategies have incorporated changes in legislation, guidance and plans. Their aims are to create a safe environment in which all children can fulfill their potential, and ensure that those in contact with them are aware of their responsibilities to promote children's welfare. The sports sector clearly has a significant role to play in meeting these aims.

For example, in England there are now clear statutory duties on all organisations that provide services for children to take steps to safeguard the welfare of all children and young people (this includes the sports sector, whether operating on a voluntary, private or local authority basis).

These national strategies and changes reflect a significant cultural shift in emphasis. The previous focus, which was on children identified as having experienced, or being at risk of, abuse (protecting children), has been widened to ensure that organisations adopt an approach to meeting the needs of all children (safeguarding). An organisation's approach to safeguarding and promoting children's welfare will demonstrate that they are: child-focused; accountable; committed to working in partnership (with children, parents and other agencies); and are giving particular attention to the needs of vulnerable children (including those who may be at risk of abuse).

Information about the strategies, legislation and guidance in place or being developed in England, Northern Ireland, Scotland and Wales can be found in Appendix C.

Many governing bodies of sport, county sports partnerships and some local authority leisure services departments are implementing safeguarding and child protection action or implementation plans. This resource will identify some of the ways your club or organisation is, or should be, operating. For example, there should be: a clear process for vetting and recruiting staff or volunteers whose roles include contact with, or responsibility for, children or young people; identified club/organisation welfare officers with a clear job description; codes of conduct for coaches, participants and carers; systems to deal with unacceptable behaviour; clear reporting procedures should concerns about possible abuse or poor practice arise (whether inside or outside the club/organisation environment); guidance on photography, transporting young athletes and away trips; and so on. A number of these practice issues are considered in greater detail in this resource.

[1] NSPCC figures, based on statistics for England, Northern Ireland and Wales.

Support to develop and implement club or organisational safeguarding and child protection policies and procedures can be accessed from the relevant governing body of sport, the Child Protection in Sport Unit or from CHILDREN 1ST in Scotland (details on pages 82–83).

This resource, and the workshop it supports, have been developed and updated to comply with current government legislation and guidance.

sports coach UK is committed to raising awareness of, and implementing action plans for, safeguarding and child protection in sport. Where there are differences in legislation and guidance across the UK, these are referenced in the resource. For further information, contact the Child Protection in Sport Unit or CHILDREN 1ST.

The emphasis of *Safeguarding and Protecting Children: A guide for sportspeople* is on coaching children. However, the pack is aimed at all those with responsibility for the organisation of children's sport (eg those working within governing bodies of sport, local authorities, sports and leisure centres and sports clubs) and those who lead or deliver children's sport programmes (eg coaches, leaders, teachers, instructors, development officers, officials, administrators, volunteers, parents)[2] – an estimated 85% of whom undertake these roles on a voluntary basis. The pack contains principles and practice guidelines that can be applied by everyone who is involved with children in a sports environment, regardless of their specific role or title.

This pack is **not** intended as an expert's comprehensive manual. Instead, it offers a practical guide for all those involved in providing sport for children. It aims to increase awareness about safeguarding and child protection, help you to recognise the signs of abuse and poor practice and subsequently deal sensitively and effectively with any issues that arise. It also prompts you to review your own practice to ensure that sport provides a positive and enriching experience for children, and that your behaviour is always above reproach.

By the end of this pack, you should be able to:

- identify the foundations of safeguarding, good practice and child protection

- describe the different categories of child abuse and the impact of abuse on children

- recognise the signs and symptoms of each category

- identify the appropriate action to take if abuse is suspected

- recognise the roles and responsibilities of relevant statutory agencies.

In the context of coaching, *Safeguarding and Protecting Children: A guide for sportspeople* will encourage you to consider the issues you may encounter when coaching children and, most importantly, to explore what good coaching practice involves. The pack also supports a three-hour sports coach UK workshop, 'Safeguarding and Protecting Children' (formerly 'Good Practice and Child Protection')[3], which you are strongly recommended to attend. This will help you put the theory behind safeguarding and child protection into practice, applying it to your own coaching.

You may have had some training and/or experience in safeguarding or child protection already. In this case, this pack will help you to think more about your responsibilities in sport settings and how you may share your knowledge and experience with others. However, you may have had no previous experience in this area and may want to spend more time on some sections than others, or discuss issues with your colleagues.

Although this pack is designed for you to work through on your own or as a follow-up to the accompanying workshop, some of the issues covered may raise strong feelings for you. It might be helpful to identify someone who is also working through the pack with whom you can meet regularly to share your thoughts. Make sure you have a clear agreement about how you will work together. Additionally, if you are unsure about the issues raised, you should make a note and discuss these with relevant staff in your club/organisation (eg club welfare officer, lead child protection officer, director of coaching, line or centre manager) or seek further support from the agencies listed in Section 4.2.

While this resource is specifically focused on safeguarding and protecting children and young people in sport, the principles of best practice should apply to all participants (including vulnerable adults), who should equally be assured a safe and enjoyable experience.

---

[2] In the context of this pack, the term *coach* is used to refer to any of the groups of people listed in this paragraph.
[3] For further details, contact the sports coach UK Workshop Booking Centre on 0845-601 3054.

- The term 'children' is used throughout this pack to refer to children and young people under the age of 18 years.*

- The term 'parents' is used throughout this pack to refer to parents, carers and legal guardians.

- In the context of this pack, the term 'governing body of sport' is used to refer to all organisations with responsibility for overseeing the policies and affairs of sport.

- Throughout this pack, the pronouns 'he', 'she', 'him', 'her' and so on are interchangeable and intended to be inclusive of both males and females.

- It is important in sport, as elsewhere, that both genders have equal status and opportunities.

- A 'vunerable adult' according to the 'Who Decides?' (HM Government, 1997) document, is 'a person aged 18 years or over who is, or may be, in need of community care services by reason of mental, or other, disability, age or illness, and who is, or may be unable to take care of him or herself, or unable to protect him or herself against significant harm or exploitation'.**

- The term 'social services' is used throughout the pack and includes the emerging children's social care departments in England and Wales. See page 68 for further details.

* There are several definitions of a 'child' in Scottish legislation. Generally, a child is a person under the age of 16 (Children [Scotland] Act 1995). In some circumstances, however, a child is defined as being under the age of 18 (eg a 16 or 17-year-old who is the subject of a supervision requirement through the Children's Hearing System). The Protection of Children (Scotland) Act 2003 also defines as child as being under 18.

** In Scotland, no legal definition of a 'vulnerable adult' exists. It has become a common term used to describe adults who may be more vulnerable to harm or abuse because of a condition, illness or ageing. In Scotland, legal definitions of an adult protected by existing legislation (eg Adults with Incapacity) can apply from the age of 16. Further guidance can be found within each local authority's local guidelines and procedures for protecting vulnerable adults, usually produced by social work departments.

SECTION ONE – The Foundations of Safeguarding, Good Practice and Child Protection **1**

SECTION TWO – Understanding and Identifying Signs of Child Abuse **27**

SECTION THREE – Taking Appropriate Action **59**

Contents

1.0 Introduction

Sport can have a very powerful and positive influence on people – especially children – and should provide opportunities for both enjoyment and achievement. Through sport, children can develop valuable qualities, such as leadership, confidence and self-esteem.

However, these positive outcomes can only be achieved if your organisation or club has prioritised safeguarding the welfare of young participants, and if the coaching you provide is of the highest possible standard. It is essential that you understand and act on your responsibilities, so that children can enjoy sport within a safe and secure environment where they feel protected and empowered to make the most suitable choices. Providing children with positive sporting experiences means that they will be more likely to achieve their true potential.

This first section will introduce you to the key principles of good coaching practice and relate these specifically to the context of coaching children. As you work through the section, you may well identify aspects of good practice that you already adopt in your work; you may also encounter other issues that have not occurred to you before, but which you may need to address when coaching children in the future.

By the end of this section, you should be able to explain the:

- key principles of sports coach UK's *Code of Practice for Sports Coaches*

- implications of these principles for:
  - coaching in general
  - your club/organisation
  - coaching children.

1.1 Code of Practice for Sports Coaches

In any profession, whether paid or voluntary, there are accepted and established codes of behaviour. For example, doctors and solicitors are required to conform to a professional code of practice. Many companies and organisations now adopt customer charters (eg The Patient's Charter, in the case of the NHS) to ensure the needs of the customer are kept paramount at all times. Such codes exist to safeguard the welfare of the customer and to protect the service provider from allegations.

A code of practice is just as necessary in coaching as in any other profession. This was first recognised by the National Coaching Foundation[4] in 1995 with the publication of its *Code of Ethics and Conduct for Sports Coaches*, which was based on an original code drawn up by the British Institute of Sports Coaches. Revised in 2001, this subsequently became sports coach UK's *Code of Practice for Sports Coaches*. The following extract from the revised code emphasises the need for a code of practice in coaching:

> *Coaching, as an emerging profession, must demonstrate at all levels a high degree of honesty, integrity and competence. The need for coaches to understand and act on their responsibilities is of critical importance to sport, as is the need to protect the key concept of participation for fun and enjoyment as well as achievement. This is implicit within good coaching practice and promotes a professional image of the good practitioner. This code of practice defines all that is best in good coaching practice.*

Code of Practice for Sports Coaches (2005)[5]

The *Code of Practice for Sports Coaches* has been adopted by a number of governing bodies of sport and by educational providers of both academic and vocational sports courses. All sports coach UK members[6] must agree to abide by the *Code* themselves, as well as to promote it to all others involved in coaching.

---

[4] Known as sports coach UK since April 2001.

[5] Available from Coachwise 1st4sport (Tel: 0113-201 5555 or visit www.1st4sport.com).

[6] sports coach UK membership services provide access to benefits and information for anyone with an interest in sport and coaching, and additional specific benefits for qualified sports coaches. For further details, telephone 0113-290 7612 or visit www.sportscoachuk.org

The *Code* is based around the four key principles described below:

> ### Code of Practice for Sports Coaches – Key Principles
>
> **Rights** – Coaches must respect and champion the rights of every individual to participate in sport.
>
> **Relationships** – Coaches must develop a relationship with athletes (and others) based on openness, honesty, mutual trust and respect.
>
> **Responsibilities: personal standards** – Coaches must demonstrate proper personal behaviour and conduct at all times.
>
> **Responsibilities: professional standards** – To maximise benefits and minimise the risks to athletes, coaches must attain a high level of competence by attaining qualifications and through a commitment to ongoing training that ensures safe and correct practice.

These key principles relate to the relationship between coaches and performers. They may also apply to relationships with other people, including parents, guardians, friends, peers, teachers, medics and the press. This list should be an active one, changing as the coaching process develops and as coaches view each performer within their individual sporting environment.

The key principles apply in any coaching situation, whatever the specific role of coaches within their club/organisation, but are particularly important when coaching children. However, they do not apply exclusively to coaches, but to all those working with children in a sporting environment.

1.2 Implications for Coaching

Section 1.1 introduced you to the four key principles of sports coach UK's *Code of Practice for Sports Coaches*. This section will explore the implications of these principles for coaching.

While the principles affect coaching in general, they are particularly important when coaching children. Children, therefore, feature in some of the scenarios in the activities so that you can start to focus on this area of coaching. In the activities, you will be asked to evaluate the actions of coaches in specific scenarios, as well as consider what you would do in other certain situations. As a result, you should begin to think about how to integrate the four key principles into your own coaching practice.

Rights

In order to respect and champion the rights of every individual to participate in sport, you should:

- provide choices for individual performers in your sport or activity

- provide an environment in which children are free from fear or harassment

- recognise the rights of performers to be treated as individuals

- encourage performers to confer with other coaches or experts if the need arises

- promote the concept of a well-balanced lifestyle for performers, both within and outside sport.

ACTIVITY 1

The aim of this activity is to focus your thoughts on player rights. In each of the scenarios in the table opposite, the coach seems to have forgotten how to be a professional. Consider how he or she could have handled the situation better and note your ideas in the right-hand column.

	Scenario	More Acceptable Solution
1	Ali books a place on a tennis course. On arriving at the first session, it's obvious that the course is very popular and that all the courts are already full. The coach looks a bit flustered and sends Ali away to play rounders until a court becomes available. He doesn't appear to have a register – in fact, he doesn't really seem familiar with the tennis course programme at all.	
2	Sandra's mother signs her up for a girls-only swimming class, as she doesn't want Sandra to take part in a mixed class. However, due to a lack of pool availability, the coach combines the girls-only class with a mixed club-training session. She thinks it will be possible to run both sessions at the same time, without the groups getting in each other's way.	
3	Moya needs to take time out from a busy training schedule to observe a religious festival. His coach is not pleased and says that Moya will lose his place in the team as a result. Several other team members also have religious festivals to observe, but feel unable to say so. The coach doesn't provide an alternative for the children concerned and says that she is not prepared to tolerate those who do not put their training first.	
4	After a close match, Jimmy is blamed for the team losing. His coach later tells other team members that Jimmy is overweight and should go on a diet.	
5	After a tournament, a coach provides feedback that reduces many of her team members to tears. They were up against some stiff competition and played as well as possible. The other teams all hear what is said and feel embarrassed for them.	

See page 85 for activity feedback.

You may feel that there are further issues to consider in relation to player rights – include these in your club/organisation's own code of practice.[7]

Relationships

As a coach, you must develop relationships with children and others that are based on openness, honesty, mutual trust and respect.

You should always:

- consider your behaviour – do not engage in behaviour that constitutes any form of abuse

- promote the welfare and best interests of your performers, even if this means letting another professional take over

- take action if you have a concern about the behaviour of an adult or young person towards a child

- empower performers to be responsible for their own decisions

- clarify the nature of the coaching services being offered to performers

- ensure the best interests of your performers when communicating and cooperating with other organisations and individuals.

You should never:

- engage in sexual intimacy with performers at any time, or under any circumstances, including immediately after the coaching relationship has ended.

[7] See page 2 for further details.

ACTIVITY 2

The aim of this activity is to apply the relationship principles described above to your own coaching environment. Consider how you would approach in your sport each of the aspects of coaching listed in the left-hand column of the table below and note your ideas in the right-hand column. An example of each aspect is provided in the middle column to help you put it into the context of coaching children.

Note: Remember that what constitutes good practice in one sport may be deemed inappropriate in another. You may need to consult with the relevant governing body of sport or seek further clarification from a sport-specific development officer. If necessary, explain how the code of practice or guidelines would vary for different performance levels and in different sports.

Aspect of Coaching	Example	Your Specific Code of Practice or Guidelines
Physical Contact	For safety reasons, you may need to lift or support a child as he performs a particular technique – your governing body of sport should be able to provide specific guidelines.	
Training Practices	Your sport may require children to participate in weight-bearing activities – your governing body of sport should be able to provide specific guidelines.	
Language	You may need to use technical language that is difficult for children to either understand or use – it's a good idea to provide a glossary of terms that they can refer to.	
Player Welfare	You may need to consider issues such as player diet or consumption of alcohol – it's a good idea to discuss this with children's parents or carers.	
Coaching Services	You could find that a child needs medical treatment after taking part in your training session – it's a good idea to meet their parents or carers to discuss issues such as recommended sports therapists or training implications.	

See page 86 for activity feedback.

© sports coach UK

Responsibilities

You will often find yourself in positions of considerable influence – particularly when coaching children. You therefore have a profound responsibility to demonstrate and set high moral and ethical standards throughout your coaching practice. Your primary role is to improve performance and to demonstrate proper personal behaviour and conduct at all times.

> **Remember!**
>
> You should always:
>
> - be fair, honest and considerate to performers and others in your sport
> - project an image of health, cleanliness and functional efficiency
> - be a positive role model for performers at all times.

ACTIVITY 3

As a coach, you have a responsibility to review and examine your behaviour constantly to ensure that it conforms to good practice and that it cannot be misconstrued.

1   With reference to responsibility and professional standards, jot down the issues you would expect to consider both before and during a coaching session in the left-hand column of the table below.

2   In the right-hand column, note the action you would take (ie what you would do and/or think about) to ensure good practice.

Issues to Consider	Action Required

See page 86 for activity feedback.

Summary

Good coaching practice involves:

- promoting safe and correct practice in relation to:
  - physical environment
  - other performers
  - significant others (eg umpires, drivers, ground staff).
- accepting professional responsibility for your actions
- making a commitment to provide a high-quality service
- providing a positive benefit to society through sport
- acknowledging that sport is a developing profession and that it is important to exchange knowledge and best practice tips
- working towards attaining coaching qualifications at different levels.

The table below lists four key actions that will help to ensure good practice in your coaching, together with examples.

You may like to share your thoughts and ideas with other professionals, colleagues and friends. The process of providing good practice in coaching is a continually developing one and depends on the cooperation and dedication of others.

Action	Examples
Follow governing body of sport/employer guidelines.	<ul><li>Attend courses.</li><li>Gather essential information.</li><li>Keep abreast of new developments.</li><li>Maintain professional level of coaching.</li><li>Make use of educational opportunities.</li><li>Comply with safeguarding and child protection requirements and procedures.</li></ul>
Locate support services in your area.	Contact:<ul><li>other clubs/coaches</li><li>sports development officers</li><li>injury/treatment experts</li><li>specific experts (eg elite level or disability sport)</li><li>local/national squads</li><li>trial organisers</li><li>schools.</li></ul>
Check your own coaching practice.	Review:<ul><li>appraisals/analysis</li><li>mentor system</li><li>session planning</li><li>workload</li><li>home demands</li><li>own health/lifestyle.</li></ul>
Review the social issues surrounding your sport.	<ul><li>Source local, regional or national initiatives.</li><li>Enquire about methods of fund-raising/grants/Lottery funding.</li><li>Reward teams and individuals.</li><li>Research training weekends, camps and tours.</li></ul>

1.3 Implications for Your Club/Organisation

This section outlines measures your club/organisation can take to promote the key principles outlined in Sections 1.1 and 1.2, and thus provide a safe sporting environment for children.

Developing a Code of Practice

In the UK, steps are being taken to ensure that codes of conduct are incorporated into governing bodies of sport and employer constitutions. Opportunities are now available for an individual, club/organisation or local authority to fully implement good practice within their coaching programmes. This may involve:

- an accreditation process

- a coach education programme

- a commitment to implement policies and procedures

- accessing central information systems (eg local authorities, governing bodies of sport, criminal records checks).

Use the key principles of sports coach UK's *Code of Practice for Sports Coaches* as the basis for a code of practice for your club/organisation:

- Begin with a policy statement that recognises the four key principles that were introduced in Section 1.1.

- Outline the importance of relationships among all those involved in the coaching process and relate these to your club/organisation's environment.

- If appropriate, involve others, such as: parents, welfare or child protection officers, volunteers, teachers and, for elite performers, advanced coaches. You should also consult your performers to help decide exactly what is acceptable and what is not.

- Amend and update your code regularly to ensure that sport continues to be a safe and fun experience for all those involved.

- Consider developing separate codes of conduct for different groups of people (eg players, referees, umpires, parents, and supporters).

Complying with codes of conduct should be a requirement, and not an option, for individuals in the relevant group. It is important that clubs/organisations have, or put in place, a policy and procedure to respond to breaches of their codes of conduct; without this, the management of concerns about an individual's behaviour can become very difficult. Most governing bodies of sport, local authorities and county sports partnerships have introduced complaints and disciplinary procedures to deal with such situations, which should be adopted and operated at all levels of the organisation.

Inevitably, all codes of conduct have their limitations – to be effective, the key principles must be acknowledged and adopted by all those involved. The aim of the next activity is to illustrate the importance of ensuring that good practice is embedded within the working practices of your entire club/organisation. Taking responsibility for this will not only help your club/organisation to promote a professional image, but is also vital to the future of sport.

ACTIVITY 4

In the space provided below, draw a diagram that identifies all the people within your club/organisation who you would need to consult when relating the key code of practice principles (outlined in Section 1.1) to the context of coaching children. It may help to place the child at the centre of your diagram. Then consider everyone who will come into direct or indirect contact with the child.

See page 87 for activity feedback.

Recruitment, Employment and Deployment of Staff

As part of its approach to safeguarding children, your club/organisation should have a robust recruitment and selection policy and procedure. This should ensure that all reasonable steps will be taken to prevent unsuitable people from working with children. The checklist below and on page 12 covers the main issues to consider when recruiting staff or volunteers.

Checklist for the Recruitment, Employment and Deployment of Staff and Volunteers

Pre-recruitment

1 Determine the aims of your club/organisation and, if possible, the particular sports programme that you wish to staff.

2 Identify the responsibilities that the member of staff will be expected to have.

3 Determine the level of experience or qualifications required, taking into account any governing body of sport and/or local authority guidelines.

4 Outline your club/organisation's open and positive stance on safeguarding and child protection.

5 Formalise your advertising procedure.

6 Prepare a job description; include roles and responsibilities.

7 Write a person specification.

8 Prepare an application form asking applicants to provide the following details:

- Name, address and National Insurance number.

- Relevant experience, qualifications and training.

- Past career or involvement in sport.

- A self-disclosure section to establish details of any criminal record, whether any disciplinary action has been taken against them in relation to working with children, and whether they have been subject to any social services or police investigations in relation to allegations of child abuse.

- The names of two people (not relatives) willing to provide written references that comment on the applicant's previous experience of, and suitability for, working with children – their previous employer is preferable.

- The applicant's consent to criminal record checks being undertaken, if necessary.

- The applicant's consent to abide by the club/organisation's code of practice appropriate to the position sought.

Forms should also state that failure to disclose information or subsequent failure to conform to the code of practice will result in disciplinary action and possible exclusion from the club/organisation.

Interview

In certain circumstances, it may be appropriate to conduct a formal interview. Ensure that it is conducted in accordance with an appropriate interview protocol.

Checks

- A minimum of two written references should be requested, one of which should be from a previous employer. All references should be followed up and confirmed by telephone.

- If the applicant has qualifications, ask to see appropriate evidence (eg certificates).

- If the applicant has no previous experience of working with children, recommend that they seek appropriate training.

- You may wish to conduct criminal record checks to assess the suitability of the applicant to work with children. This can be done via the:

  - criminal records checks (England and Wales)[8]

  - Disclosure Scotland (Scotland)

  - DHSSPS Pre-Employment Consultancy Service (PECS) (Northern Ireland).

- A number of governing bodies of sport are establishing centralised systems to access CRB checks for staff and volunteers, which you may be able to access.

Training

- Ensure that all new members of staff receive a formal induction to your club/organisation (eg introduction to your facility and basic procedures, such as fire drills, safety and first aid).

  All staff working with children are recommended to receive training in the following areas:[9]

  - Safeguarding and child protection awareness.

  - First aid.

  - Working effectively with children.

  - Child-centred coaching styles.

It is also essential that staff receive regular, follow-up training to ensure that they are kept up to date with current issues.

Monitoring and Appraisal

All staff or volunteers should be given the opportunity to receive feedback (eg at the end of a particular sports programme or at regular intervals during an ongoing programme).

Complaints

Check that your organisation or club has a formal complaints procedure.

---

[8] See Appendix A for further details.

[9] sports coach UK offers a wide range of workshops and supporting packs in a variety of coaching-related areas. Telephone 0845-601 3054 or visit www.sportscoachuk.org for further details.

ACTIVITY 5

Comment on the guidelines on pages 11 and 12 Are they realistic? Are they achievable? Could you suggest further areas for development within your organisation?

....

....

....

....

....

....

....

....

....

....

....

....

....

....

....

....

....

....

....

Communication

Good communication is vital to the effective operation of your club/organisation in general, but is particularly important in the context of coaching children.

Establishing and maintaining effective communication channels in your club/organisation could involve:

- publishing a newsletter
- producing brief outlines of key policies for players and parents
- organising fund-raising activities
- setting up a committee
- establishing a supporters' club
- setting up a Lottery panel
- establishing and maintaining a link with the local sports development officer

- providing a coach education programme
- providing in-house training/ development opportunities.

Many clubs/organisations have implemented systems through which they can share good practice and provide coach feedback through formal channels. With such a system in place, managers should be able to identify concerns that could be addressed by a coach education programme or a simple change of coaching focus.

Examples of Good Practice

The next activity asks you to identify examples of good practice at a fictional sports club. Some of these may already exist in your club/organisation; others may be things you hadn't necessarily thought of before.

© Alan Edwards

ACTIVITY 6

Read through the following scenario. As you do, jot down any examples of good practice that you come across.

A number of improvements have been made to Parkgate Sports Club over the past few months. These include the installation of a free drinking-water fountain, a telephone from which club members can make free local calls, security lighting and the services of a night security agency.

The club committee already runs a number of activity schemes and systematically reviews both the quality and scope of provision. All committee members have attended a range of sports administration courses and support the various activity schemes in their capacity as volunteer coaches. The club was recently awarded Clubmark status. The full-time coaching officer is responsible for planning a programme of activities for the entire summer holiday, ensuring adequate staffing arrangements, and for the behaviour and standards of the club's coaches.

The next plan of action is to organise a sports play scheme during a school holiday for local children aged seven to 14. At the first committee meeting, roles and responsibilities are allocated to committee members in order to recruit staff to provide a range of indoor and outdoor activities.

An advert is subsequently placed in a local newspaper. All applicants are required to complete an application form, attend an interview, supply two references, and agree to a criminal records check being undertaken, if they are offered the post. All successful applicants are asked to attend formal induction programmes at the club and are employed on short-term contracts.

With all staff members and volunteers recruited, children are invited to enrol on the play scheme. All of them are asked to complete appropriate registration documents and to attend an orientation session, during which club rules and regulations are explained. Parents are invited to attend at least one orientation session per family of children and to meet all club staff. The club operates an inclusion policy and does all it can to cater for members' specific needs, as and when required.

Every day, one of the committee members is on duty and responsible, not just for general duties, but also for checking facilities and equipment. During activity sessions the club is closed to members of the public, with entry via a main reception area. Children also use this system to check in and leave. The club encourages parents/carers or a named person to collect their children at the end of their session. Children are invited to provide feedback (either after a specific session or on a weekly basis) and have access to non-coaching volunteers for queries. All courses are reviewed on a regular basis, in terms of attendance and quality.

See page 88 for activity feedback.

1.4 Implications for Coaching Children

It is essential that a culture of honesty, integrity and competence exists in coaching.

This means:

- understanding and acting on your responsibilities as a coach

- recognising the need to protect the key concept of participation for fun and enjoyment, as well as achievement.

> **Remember!**
>
> All staff, including coaches who work independently, should not only be required to sign up to your club/organisation's code of practice, but also ensure that they demonstrate good practice at all times.

© Alan Edwards

Acting as a Role Model

Not all children may behave as you would like during your coaching sessions. Often, they are influenced by the media's portrayal of their professional sports-star heroes. Unfortunately, the media tend to focus on incidents of poor, rather than good, behaviour and often blow things out of proportion. However, children are unlikely to understand this and may try to emulate undesirable behaviour that they have witnessed in major matches or events. This may result in a conflict between you and the children and, if ignored, could have disastrous consequences.

As a coach, you should always try to be a positive role model for the children you coach. If you act in a responsible manner, they will be encouraged to do so, too. Following the tips in the box below will help you to do this:

- Appearance – always project a professional image.

- Fashion – you need to wear kit and equipment that is recommended and appropriate to the activity/sport.

- Tattoos – very popular, but not always desirable.

- Jewellery – remove, or at least tape up, any jewellery during sport.

- Language – it is often not just what is said that is important, but how it is said. Never use foul language in front of the children you coach.

- Smoking – always discourage children from smoking, and set a positive example.

- Alcohol – it is unacceptable to consume, or be under the influence of, alcohol when responsible for children.

- Drugs – take a firm stance against drugs and lead by example.

ACTIVITY 7

Read through the following scenario:

Your team has reached the final of a local competition. On the day of the match, several supporters turn up to watch, so the atmosphere is noisy and the team members are very excited. You know the referee and you instruct your team to play fairly, but hard. You emphasise that the referee is tough and that they will have to watch their language, tackles and general behaviour. However, you are very pleased that they have reached this stage in the competition, and find it difficult not to concentrate just on winning.

During the first half, the score is even and the crowd is satisfied with the general play and the referee's decisions. However, late in this half, due to a poor tackle from a member of the other team, your best player has to leave the pitch injured. Soon after this, the other team scores and takes the lead. You see that your players are demoralised, tired and desperate to equalise. It is at this point that you notice the standard of their play deteriorates – you also spot incidents of shirt pulling, late tackles and offensive language.

In the space provided below, explain what you would do during half-time to re-focus your players. What would you say to them?

....

....

....

....

....

....

....

....

....

....

....

....

....

See page 88 for activity feedback.

Empowering Children

As a coach – particularly of children – you hold a powerful and unique leadership role, often carrying considerable authority and status. This role is frequently accompanied by a closeness and mutual trust usually held only between the parent and the child. You often wittingly or unwittingly assume this level of authority and, occasionally, your influence spills over into the child's personal life. One of the challenges you repeatedly face is to manage this potential power and to balance the responsible and safe boundary between coach and performer. The challenge to do this is exacerbated by the need for you to build high levels of trust from children – particularly those involved in elite performance – in order to encourage them to optimise their performance and develop the level of commitment required to achieve their potential.

When coaching children, you may start by using your authoritative role to build a strong relationship or bond. This can, and often does, result in you having a very positive influence over the child – sometimes an influence that grows even more powerful than that of the child's parents or schoolteachers. Over time, the all-important trust needed normally develops.

However, with this trust comes increased vulnerability and the potential for you to misuse, or even abuse, your power. This might be the result of thoughtlessness, negligence or, occasionally, wickedness. Even a passive type of abuse of power (for example, by questioning a child's loyalty or commitment) may sharpen the child's need for belonging. Over time, this may result in over-conformity, obsessive behaviours and emotional dependency.

As you become an important figure for a child, you may need to examine your own coaching behaviour. Likewise, the child may develop an inappropriate attachment to you, based on a misunderstanding or misreading of your relationship. Care should be taken to ensure that the relationship is an appropriate and positive one, and not one that could be open to abuse or misinterpretation. In this way, you will help to protect the child and yourself, and provide a positive role model for other coaches and children.

There is, of course, a close but potentially dangerous relationship between commitment and conformity. Inadvertently or intentionally, you may encourage conformity to your values and ideals of commitment to sport. In seeking greater sporting commitment, you may, therefore, be over-stressing the need to conform and so possibly thwarting personal responsibility and self-determination, thus encouraging over-dependence in the child. It is important to recognise and avoid the potential negative consequences of power and trust. Your role as a coach should be to instil confidence in the children you coach, so that they are willing to play an active role in the coaching process.

© Andrew Orchard

Figure 1 below illustrates the constituents of responsible leadership. Try to relate it to your own coaching. How well do you manage your relationships with your own performers?

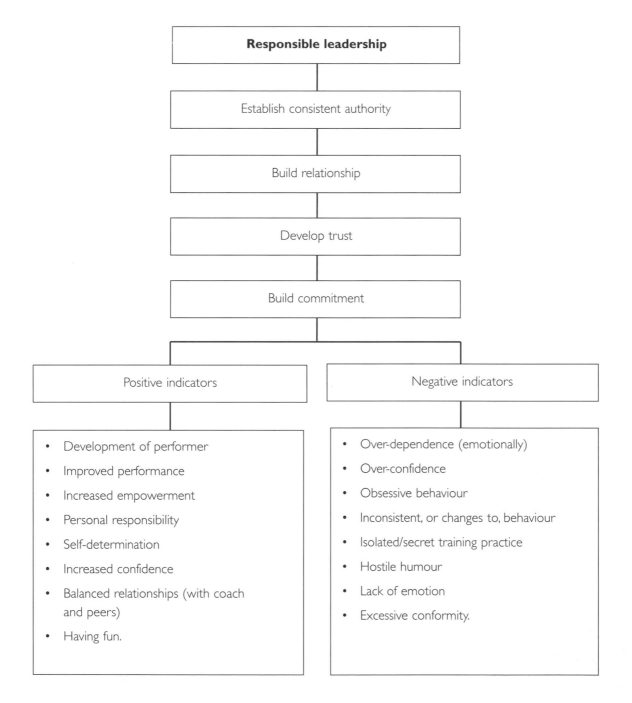

Figure 1: Responsible leadership

Adopting Good Practice

You should try to compile a list of actions that will help you become child-focused and ensure good practice and standards. This should be an active list and should be constantly updated, in line with the changing coaching environment, a variety of social needs, your own expectations and the demands of others.

ACTIVITY 8

The good practice toolbox in the left-hand column of the table below contains examples of good practice that you should try to adopt in your coaching practice.

In the right-hand column, jot down ways in which you could do this. If you can, add extra examples of good practice in the spaces provided at the end of the table (on page 21).

Good Practice Toolbox	Action Points
Make sport fun and enjoyable, and promote fair play.	
Always give enthusiastic and constructive feedback.	
Treat everyone fairly and with respect and dignity.	
Build balanced relationships based on mutual trust.	
Empower children to make their own decisions.	
Be an excellent role model – in your behaviour, attitude and appearance.	
Work in an open environment – avoid closed, unobserved situations.	
Listen to children and invite their opinion of your coaching.	
Keep up-to-date with technical skills, insurance and qualifications.	

Acknowledge the diverse contributions that sport science can make to the coaching process.	
Observe the relevant governing body of sport's guidelines on contact/manual support of children and explain them to children and their parents/carers.	
Involve parents/carers in the supervision of children.	
Carry out risk assessments and complete appropriate paperwork.	
Keep accurate and up-to-date records.	
Plan ahead for tournaments and competitions.	
Ensure adequate staffing for away events in line with club, governing body of sport and local authority guidelines.	
Review transport arrangements for staff and performers.	
Check all kit and equipment frequently for signs of wear and tear.	
Identify when to have a break from coaching responsibilities.	
Practice emergency situations (eg fire, injury).	

Add any extra examples of good practice that you can think of in the space provided below.

Poor Practice

As well as adopting and promoting good practice, it is also important to recognise and respond to examples of poor practice (ie actions that fail to comply with the key principles of good practice and child protection). These could include:

- rough, physical and/or sexually provocative games

- inappropriate touching

- children using inappropriate language without being challenged

- children being reduced to tears as a form of control

- the use of sexually suggestive comments, even in jest

- failing to respond to allegations made by a child.

This list is not exhaustive and you may be able to identify additional examples. In all cases, poor practice must be challenged and attempts made to rectify the situation.

Use team meetings to discuss actual and potential examples of good and poor practice. This will help to foster an open and positive sporting environment.

Recognising and Correcting Poor Practice

You may think that you already have a responsible attitude towards your role as a coach. This may well be the case, but what evidence do you have of this? The following activity asks you to evaluate and reflect on specific coaching scenarios in which you would need to demonstrate responsible and professional practice.

ACTIVITY 9

Read through each of the following scenarios. In the spaces provided, note down:

a) any views or concerns you may have

b) a possible solution to the situation.

1   A gifted young performer in an under-14s squad requests individual, one-to-one coaching, even though they are part of a group.

a   Your views/concerns:

....

....

....

b   Possible solution:

....

....

....

2   Some children whom you coach ask to visit your house to see your collection of sports medals and trophies, and to borrow some training manuals.

   a   Your views/concerns:

   . . . .

   . . . .

   . . . .

   b   Possible solution:

   . . . .

   . . . .

   . . . .

3   You are asked to attend a training weekend where, for supervisory purposes, you are allocated a sleeping area with a group of children.

   a   Your views/concerns:

   . . . .

   . . . .

   . . . .

   b   Possible solution:

   . . . .

   . . . .

   . . . .

4   A new coach uses inappropriate language which the children repeat, making fun of other groups in a loud, suggestive manner.

   a   Your views/concerns:

   . . . .

   . . . .

   . . . .

b   Possible solution:

....

....

....

5   You are asked to coach a young adult with special needs, but are not given time to discuss her specific personal requirements, either with the young adult herself or her carer.

a   Your views/concerns:

....

....

....

b   Possible solution:

....

....

....

6   A child in your care receives a bang to his head. He appears to be fine and you forget to inform his parents and omit to complete an accident report.

a   Your views/concerns:

....

....

....

b   Possible solution:

....

....

7   During a coaching session, a young performer begins to suggest that they really like you and would like to meet you for a coffee.

a   Your views/concerns:

. . . .

. . . .

. . . .

b   Possible solution:

. . . .

. . . .

. . . .

8   You are asked to take a squad to an away fixture by yourself.

a   Your views/concerns:

. . . .

. . . .

. . . .

b   Possible solution:

. . . .

. . . .

. . . .

See page 88 for activity feedback.

Poor practice can be harmful for participants, coaches and the club or organisation. It provides a negative model of behaviour and attitude for others, and may lead to misconceptions about the motivation and intent of those involved. It may contribute to creating an environment in which other inappropriate behaviour is accepted or can flourish. Most seriously, poor practice may be part of the grooming process (see page 37) employed by an individual who is motivated to abuse a child.

Sound recruitment processes, the application of codes of practice and prompt reporting of, and responses to, concerns can all contribute to eradicating poor practice and reducing these associated risks.

1.5 Summary

In this first section, you have been introduced to four key principles relating to good coaching practice:

- Rights

- Relationships

- Responsibilities: personal standards

- Responsibilities: professional standards.

You have also considered these principles in the context of coaching children and should now understand the crucial role you play in the development of sport and in the lives of the children you coach.

You should also have begun to think about the issues arising from the key principles and the action required to address them. Good practice involves ensuring that these actions result in a professional approach to coaching where there is evidence of honesty, integrity and competence. The aim is to provide sporting opportunities for children – for fun as well as for achievement – within a safe and secure environment.

For further information relating to some of the issues explored in this section, the following sports coach UK leaflets are particularly recommended:[10]

- *Code of Practice for Sports Coaches* (2005)

- *Safe and Sound* (updated 2005).

In the next section, you will start to address the issues surrounding child abuse in general and, in particular, concerns arising in sport. Examine your own feelings as you work through it. Initially, you may believe it has nothing to do with you because you think child abuse does not happen in your sport. Alternatively, you may accept that it occurs, but feel this material is irrelevant because it does not apply to your own behaviour (or that of your peer-group coaches). For some of you, the material may arouse a strong emotional reaction, perhaps because you have been abused yourself, know someone who has, or have concerns about a particular child or adult with whom you sometimes work. Whatever your initial feelings, you will not be alone. You may also find that your attitude or feelings change as you work through the pack.

© Alan Edwards

[10] Both leaflets are available from Coachwise 1st4sport (Tel: 0113-201 5555 or visit www.1st4sport.com).

2.0 Introduction

All those directly or indirectly involved with children's sport have a responsibility to:

- identify their values and feelings in relation to child abuse, and recognise how they may impact on their responses

- be able to recognise and respond to signs and indicators of child abuse.

Even for those experienced in working with child abuse, it is not always easy to recognise situations where abuse has already taken place or may potentially occur. As a coach, you are not expected to be an expert, but you do have a responsibility to act if you have any concerns about the behaviour of an adult or a child towards another child.

In this section, you will be given the opportunity to explore what child abuse is and to consider your own feelings, beliefs and values in relation to it. Through the use of case studies, you will begin to differentiate categories of abuse and will then be encouraged to start to recognise the signs and indicators. Although quite factual, this section is intended to stimulate both thought and discussion. By the end of the section, you should be able to:

- consider your own beliefs and preconceived ideas about child abuse

- describe the different categories of child abuse

- describe the effects of abuse

- describe the incidence of abuse and identify those children most at risk

- identify the signs and symptoms of child abuse in sports situations.

2.1 What Constitutes Child Abuse?

The term 'child abuse' is used to describe all the ways in which children are harmed, usually by adults and often by those they know and trust. It refers to the damage that has been, or may be, done to a child's physical or mental health or development. This may occur at home, at school or in a community setting, including a sports environment. An adult may abuse a child both by inflicting harm and by failing to prevent harm. Alternatively, a child may abuse another child – indeed, there is growing evidence to suggest that peer abuse is an increasing concern for young people.

Some adults and young people who are motivated to harm children deliberately seek out opportunities to work or volunteer in environments that offer access to young people. This may include education and social care settings (eg schools or residential homes) or other community settings (eg youth or sports clubs). It is therefore important that any organisations or groups that provide services for children and young people have effective recruitment and deployment systems in place. This process is designed to limit access to children and young people by those known or believed to represent a risk to them, and should include seeking appropriate references and criminal records checks (see pages 68–69 and Appendix A).

The following activity is designed to begin to address your own feelings when faced with an incident of potential child abuse.

ACTIVITY 10

Read through the following scenario:

At the end of a coaching session, you dismiss your group of children and escort them to the changing area. Outside the changing rooms, you notice several parents waiting to collect their children and go across to join them. As the children reappear from the changing rooms, you notice one mum looking cross as her son George trails various items of clothing across the floor, dropping a pile of clothes at her feet. George's mum has parked on a double yellow line and can see a traffic warden approaching.

George struggles to put his kit in his bag and can't find one of his trainers. His mum pushes him back quite harshly in the direction of the changing rooms and shouts at him to hurry up. You notice there are two other children in George's mum's car, both of whom appear to be crying.

When George finally emerges from the changing rooms with his missing trainer, his mum is having a lively discussion with the traffic warden who, despite her pleas, gives her a parking ticket. George attempts to get in the car, but is stopped by his mum who continues to shout and blames him for the parking fine. The last you see is George rubbing his head as he fumbles with his seat belt.

Now jot down your initial feelings:

....

....

....

....

....

....

....

....

....

....

....

....

See page 89 for activity feedback.

Try to identify what you understand by the term 'abuse' by assessing the situations in the following activity.

ACTIVITY 11

Remember!

Defining child abuse is made more difficult because of each person's different values and ideas about what constitutes child abuse. Most of the statements below do not provide enough information for you to determine whether the behaviour constitutes neglect or abuse.

However, as a coach, **it is not your responsibility to decide.** Your role is to be aware of possible indicators of abuse in order to inform others appropriately.

Consider which of the following behaviours between children and adults are acceptable and which are not, and identify your reason(s)[11]:

1   A four-year-old child being left alone for half an hour.

    Not acceptable/acceptable . . . .

    . . . .

    Reason(s) . . . .

    . . . .

2   A 12-year-old child being left alone in the house for the evening.

    Not acceptable/acceptable . . . .

    . . . .

    Reason(s) . . . .

    . . . .

3   A five-year-old girl being sent to school in January wearing a thin cotton dress and a summer jacket.

    Not acceptable/acceptable . . . .

    . . . .

    Reason(s) . . . .

    . . . .

4   A 13-year-old boy going without lunch and dinner.

    Not acceptable/acceptable . . . .

    . . . .

    Reason(s) . . . .

    . . . .

[11] Some of these questions were adapted from an original exercise developed by the Open University in *Child Abuse and Neglect: An Introduction* (1989).

5 An instructor taking a group hillwalking without adequate clothing.

Not acceptable/acceptable ....

....

Reason(s) ....

....

6 A father smacking his 12-year-old daughter because she arrives home two hours late.

Not acceptable/acceptable ....

....

Reason(s) ....

....

7 An organisation's requirements for a particular competition cause the performer to make abnormal changes to his or her body composition/shape.

Not acceptable/acceptable ....

....

Reason(s) ....

....

8 A father bathing his 11-year-old daughter.

Not acceptable/acceptable ....

....

Reason(s) ....

....

9 A mother bathing her 10-year-old son.

Not acceptable/acceptable ....

....

Reason(s) ....

....

10 A female babysitter bathing a 10-year-old boy who is physically disabled.

Not acceptable/acceptable ....

....

Reason(s) ....

....

22 Initiation ceremonies within sports teams.

Not acceptable/acceptable . . . .

. . . .

Reason(s) . . . .

. . . .

See page 89 for activity feedback.

2.2 Truths and Myths

Having explored your feelings a little more fully, assess your current knowledge about child abuse and neglect by answering the questions in the next activity.

ACTIVITY 12

A number of commonly held views are stated below. Decide whether each is true or false:

1	Children are abused mostly by strangers.	True/False
2	It is only men who sexually abuse children.	True/False
3	Disabled children are less likely to be victims of abuse.	True/False
4	Girls are much more likely to be abused than boys.	True/False
5	In some cultures, it is acceptable for children to be abused.	True/False
6	If social services are involved, children are usually removed from their homes.	True/False
7	Children are resilient and, therefore, recover quickly from abuse.	True/False
8	Children under the age of five are more likely to be abused than older children.	True/False
9	More children are abused now than 20 years ago.	True/False
10	Children often lie about abuse.	True/False
11	There is widespread reported occurrence of abuse in sport.	True/False
12	Coaches have many opportunities to abuse children emotionally as well as physically.	True/False

See page 89 for activity feedback.

Activities 11 and 12 helped you consider some of your own beliefs and preconceived ideas about child abuse. Unless these are explored, there is a danger that your judgement may be clouded or prejudiced. It is therefore important to be open-minded at all times. Having explored your beliefs and preconceived ideas, you will now be more receptive to the following information about categories and signs of abuse.

2.3 Categories of Abuse

Child abuse can take many forms, but can be broadly separated into five main categories:

* Neglect

* Physical abuse

* Sexual abuse

* Emotional abuse

* Bullying and harassment.

Neglect

Neglect occurs when adults fail to meet a child's basic physical and/or psychological needs, and is likely to result in the serious impairment of the child's health or development. Examples of neglect include:

* failing to provide adequate food, shelter or clothing

* regularly leaving children alone or unsupervised

* failing to protect a child from physical harm or danger

* failing to ensure access to appropriate medical care or treatment

* refusing to give children affection and attention.

Examples in sport

Neglect in a sport situation could include a coach failing to ensure that children are safe and comfortable, or exposing them to undue cold or heat, or to unnecessary risk of injury.

© Alan Edwards

ACTIVITY 13

In the left-hand column of the table below, list situations in which neglect could occur in your sport. In the right-hand column, identify examples of good practice, which you undertake to ensure the safety of the children you coach.

Potential Examples of Neglect	Examples of Good Practice

Physical Abuse

Physical abuse occurs when someone causes physical harm or injury to a child. Examples include:

- hitting, shaking or throwing children
- poisoning, burning or scalding children
- biting, suffocating or drowning children
- giving children inappropriate drugs or alcohol
- otherwise causing them deliberate physical harm.

Examples in sport

Physical abuse in a sport situation may be deemed to occur if the nature and intensity of training and competition exceeds the capacity of the child's immature and growing body. This includes instances where drugs are used to delay puberty, control diet or enhance performance.

ACTIVITY 14

In the space provided below, note down questions that you could ask to identify any concerns about physical issues relating to your sport and the children you coach. An example has been given to start you off.

Example
Should I encourage children to consume high-energy drinks or tablets prior to a race during a competition?

....

....

....

....

....

....

....

....

....

....

....

....

....

....

....

....

See page 91 for activity feedback.

Sexual Abuse

Sexual abuse occurs when adults (both male and female) or other young people use children to meet their own sexual needs. This could include:

- full sexual intercourse

- masturbation, oral sex, anal intercourse or fondling

- involving children in producing pornographic material (eg videos, photographs)

- showing children pornographic material (eg magazines, videos, pictures).

Examples in sport

There are situations within all sports where the potential for this form of abuse exists:

- Some individuals have deliberately targeted sports activities in order to gain access to, and abuse, children.

- There is evidence that individuals have sometimes ignored codes of conduct, and used physical contact within a coaching role to mask their inappropriate touching of children (for example, while supporting an athlete on a piece of equipment).

- Some coaches consider it an acceptable part of the sports culture to have a sexual relationship with their young protégés.

- Some people have used sporting events as an opportunity to take inappropriate photographs or videos of sportspeople (including young and disabled participants) in vulnerable positions.

The term 'grooming' refers to the way in which sexual abusers (or potential abusers) manipulate targeted victims, carers, colleagues and their environment. They do this to make it easier to abuse children and to reduce the likelihood of the child either telling or being believed should they disclose what is happening. Grooming behaviours may appear to be positive (for example, in providing a particular child or group with extra attention/treats/lifts to and from events, or by the individual making himself highly thought of and indispensable within a club), and the plausibility of the individuals concerned often makes it difficult for others to identify their real motivation. However, they will also ignore, undermine or resist the application of good practice and other safeguarding guidelines. Adherence to codes of conduct, an understanding of acceptable/unacceptable behaviour, and an awareness on the part of everyone in a club/organisation of when and how to report concerns, will all contribute to identifying and dealing with grooming behaviours. Concerns about an adult's behaviour should be reported to the relevant club or organisation child protection officer.

© Alan Edwards

ACTIVITY 15

In the space provided below, record specific guidelines relating to physical contact in your sport. If you are not sure, contact your governing body of sport for advice and guidance.

....

....

....

....

....

....

....

....

....

....

....

....

....

....

....

....

....

....

....

....

Emotional Abuse

This is the emotional ill treatment of a child that results in severe and persistent adverse effects on his or her emotional development. Although it can occur in isolation, children who have suffered neglect or physical/sexual abuse will also have suffered some level of emotional abuse. Research shows that children who experience an emotionally abusive environment are at higher risk of suffering other forms of abuse. Children of all ages can be emotionally abused in a number of ways, such as through:

- imposing developmentally inappropriate expectations on them

- making them feel worthless, unloved, inadequate or valued only insofar as they meet the needs of another person

- making their positive self-image entirely dependent on sporting achievement and success

- making them feel frightened or in danger

- shouting at, threatening or taunting them

- overprotecting them or, conversely, failing to give them the love and affection they need.

Examples in sport

Emotional abuse may occur in sport if children are subjected to constant criticism, name-calling, sarcasm, bullying, racism or unrealistic pressure to consistently perform to high expectations. In some cases, this may come from parents and coaches. The inappropriate use or availability of personal information or images (in the media, Internet, photographs or even a club notice board) can be distressing for any performer.

As a result of emotional abuse, children may feel nervous, lack confidence and self-worth, and learn to dislike any form of activity. It is up to the coach to lead by example and to ensure that concerning incidents are handled with care and sensitivity, so that the situation is controlled and not made worse.

© Alan Edwards

ACTIVITY 16

In the diagram provided below, record the groups of people who could be responsible for subjecting a child to emotional abuse in your sport – you may wish to discuss these groups with other coaches first. An example has been given to start you off.

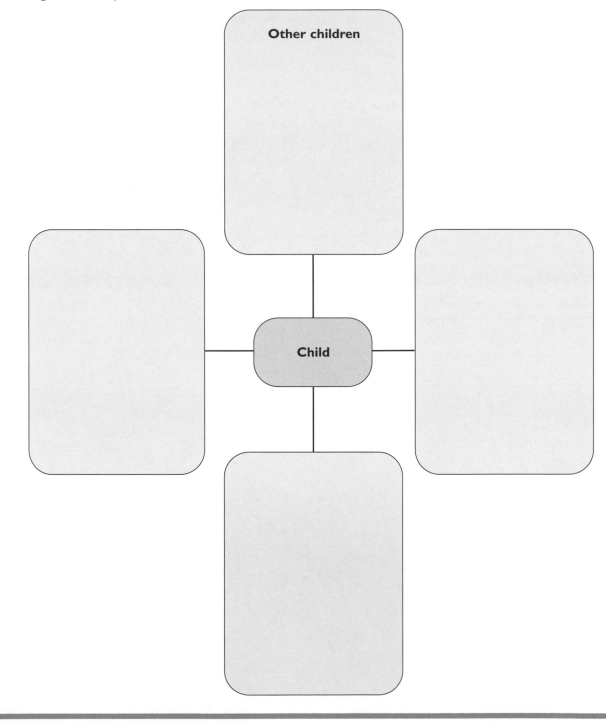

See page 91 for activity feedback.

Bullying and Harassment

Bullying is deliberately hurtful behaviour, usually repeated over a period of time, where it is difficult for those bullied to defend themselves. It can be verbal, written or physical and can include actions such as:

- physical assaults
- name-calling, sarcasm and racist taunts
- threats and gestures
- unwanted physical contact
- graffiti
- stealing or hiding personal items
- being ostracised or ignored.

Bullying can also occur via the Internet, by phone or through text messaging.

In November 2000, the NSPCC published the results of major research carried out to explore the childhood experience of young people in the UK, including their experience of abuse and neglect[12]. The survey found that:

- 43% of the young people questioned identified bullying or being discriminated against by other children as the most common source of distress or misery
- bullying occurred mostly because of personal characteristics such as size, dress, race or manner of speech
- name-calling and verbal abuse were the most common forms of bullying
- 14–15% of the young people questioned were physically attacked
- many reported having had their property stolen or damaged.

The report concludes that, for many children, the wider world of school, friends and community contains threats of bullying and discrimination and, for girls in particular, sexual harassment and violence.

Although anyone can be the target of bullying, victims are typically shy, sensitive or insecure. Sometimes they are singled out for physical reasons (eg being overweight or smaller than everyone else, having a disability, or belonging to a different race, faith or culture).

The effects of bullying may be invisible, but can leave lasting emotional scars. The bully is not always obvious to others and the victim often keeps quiet.

Harassment is closely associated with aspects of bullying and occurs when an individual feels that they are subject to behaviour from others that is unacceptable to them. Such behaviour could include simple name-calling or an action that is designed to annoy, upset or worry another child. In some cases, it may develop into an identifiable pattern of bullying; in other more subtle cases, it may take the form of random acts – again designed to upset others.

Examples in sport

The competitive nature of sport makes it an ideal environment for the bully. The bully could be:

- a parent who pushes his or her child too hard
- a coach who shouts at, or humiliates, children
- children who actively seek to make sport a difficult or unhappy experience for others.

Although bullying often takes place in schools, it can and does occur wherever there is the opportunity for children to meet (eg changing rooms, practice and social areas in sports centres, during journeys to and from sports activities). The bully may not be selective in the location, but is always likely to be careful about who else may be able to observe what is said or done. The damage inflicted by bullying is frequently underestimated. It can cause considerable distress to some children to the extent that they may stop participating in sport altogether.

Although it may be difficult for you to anticipate when your actions could provide further opportunities for the bully, you have a responsibility to ensure that sport is a positive experience for all children. Carefully observe the children you coach to evaluate whether they are being included in activities by other children and whether they have the confidence to voice any doubts they may have. It is easy to tell if children are unhappy – you cannot get the best out of them if they are hurting emotionally.

---

[12] Child Maltreatment in the United Kingdom: A Study of the Prevalence of Child Abuse and Neglect (2000).

ACTIVITY 17

1   Read through the following scenarios and decide whether they are examples of how children avoid being bullied. Indicate your response in the middle column of the table.

2   Try to work out why their behaviour is not quite what you would expect. Note your ideas in the right-hand column of the table.

Scenario	Yes/No	Reasons
1 You notice a member of a team that you coach will not get changed at the same time as everyone else. She always arrives in her kit and stays late to clear up the equipment or just to chat, so that by the time she goes into the changing rooms, everyone else is leaving. She declines the offer of a free fitness test and fails to attend a club outing to the local swimming pool. When you think about it, you realise that this child always remains fully covered for every activity and is often on her own.		
2 You hear that a new member of the team you coach is from another area of the town and that the other team members do not like him. Teams for today's game were decided last week, so the newcomer has to wait for an opportunity to join in. You decide to ask him to help referee the game and tell him he will be able to play later on. However, during the first few minutes of play, he blows the whistle and makes a controversial decision. This upsets the team members and, when the newcomer joins the team, he is left out of the play. The rest of the team members pass the ball among themselves and call the newcomer names. You notice that after the session, the team members are quiet and the atmosphere is very icy. The newcomer changes quickly and leaves.		
3 You ask a group you coach to work with an older, mixed team for training purposes. Most of the team members feel that this is an excellent idea, but some members of the group look worried. The older team contains skilled, technical players. They are bigger, heavier and have a reputation for playing very hard.		

See page 92 for activity feedback.

© sports coach UK

2.4 Effects of Abuse

The effects of child abuse can be devastating, especially if children are left unprotected or do not have access to people who can help them cope with abuse.

Adult survivors of child abuse typically say that their childhood experiences have made them feel guilty and worthless. They may have blamed themselves for what happened, which in turn led to anxiety, depression and, sometimes, difficulty in forming or maintaining relationships. If help is not provided, the behaviour displayed by children who have been abused may persist into adult life, and can sometimes lead to abusive relationships with their own children or with other adults.

As a result of abuse, children may:

- die – clearly the most serious effect

- suffer pain and distress

- develop behavioural difficulties, such as becoming angry and aggressive

- experience a developmental delay (physically, emotionally and mentally)

- experience school-related problems (eg loss of concentration, even refusing to go to school altogether)

- develop low self-esteem and lack confidence

- suffer depression or inflict self-harm, sometimes leading to suicide attempts

- become withdrawn or introverted

- suffer temporary, or even permanent, injury.

2.5 Incidence of Abuse

How many children are abused?

The following figures are taken from NSPCC **inform**, based on statistics provided by the DfES, Scottish Executive, Department of Health, Social Services and Public Safety (Northern Ireland), and the Local Government Data Unit (Wales). The child protection register indicates children who have been abused or are at serious risk of abuse.

Table 2: Estimates of national incidence of child abuse per year (includes figures for England, Scotland, Northern Ireland and Wales)

Category of Abuse	2001	2002	2003	2004	2005
Neglect	14,335	13,023	14,165	12,492	13,962
Physical abuse	9512	6112	7282	5558	5268
Sexual abuse	4981	3400	3666	3084	3037
Emotional abuse	5432	5583	6487	6182	6288
Mixed categories	772	4563	4768	4034	3474
Category unknown/not given	191				29
Total	33,223	33,181	36,559	32,450	32,056

These figures clearly demonstrate a high level of officially recorded abuse across the UK. Some changes in the rates recorded within individual categories reflect alterations in the way in which data is collated and recorded. As yet, no figures relating specifically to sport are available. However, the fact that there are a growing number of known cases of abuse in sport is evidence enough. Every possible measure should therefore be taken to ensure that sport is a safe experience for children.

Risks

Child abuse can happen to children of all ages, regardless of their gender, race, culture or background. What places children at risk of abuse?

Some children are perceived as being more vulnerable than others. Assessing the overall risk to a child is a very complex task, undertaken by child protection professionals. This process takes account of many factors such as:

- high levels of stress

- previous violence in the family

- poor relationships between parents or carers

- the age of the child

- the history and characteristics of the abuser

- potential access to the child by the abuser.

However, even when many of these factors exist, it does not necessarily mean that the child concerned will be abused.

Remember!

There are certain categories of children who may be especially at risk for various reasons:

- Very young children, and those with a physical disability or learning difficulty, may be more vulnerable to abuse. They may also find it more difficult to tell people – because of either language difficulties or limited access to people they can trust[13].

- Children from ethnic minorities who are being abused and who may also be experiencing racial discrimination, may find it hard to tell someone because they feel doubly powerless.

- Children in a sport situation may be vulnerable because of the possible use of physical contact (eg through physical demonstration, supporting movements) or through the use of emotional blackmail (eg 'It's the only way you will reach the top levels').

- There is a growing body of research and case evidence to indicate that young elite athletes are particularly vulnerable to abuse and the effects of poor coaching practice.

- Factors that increase the vulnerability of elite young athletes to abuse include: increased travel and away (overnight) trips to unfamiliar places with unfamiliar people; more frequent separation from family and friendship networks[14]; increased pressure to perform; a high level of dependence on the coach for continued sporting progress, representative squad membership and personal affirmation; and young athletes and parents recognising that there is more to lose by challenging a coach's behaviour.

Care should therefore be taken to ensure that safeguarding measures reflect the specific needs and potential vulnerabilities of these groups.

To compound the problems, adults do not always hear or pick up the messages children give to indicate that they are being abused. This places children at further risk. Abused children may also behave in ways that adults find difficult to cope with and which makes them more vulnerable. However, recent research clearly indicates that children and adults can recover from the effects of abuse if they are believed, protected from further abuse, and receive the help they need to overcome the experiences they have suffered[15].

Before moving on to the next section, you may wish to complete the following activity to check you have grasped the essential information.

© Alan Edwards

[13] Based on information from *The Abuse of Children and Adults with Disabilities* (1993).

[14] 'Safe Sports Events' Tiivas, A. and Morton, J. (2003).

[15] Further information is available on the NSPCC website (www.nspcc.org.uk).

ACTIVITY 18

1 List the main categories of child abuse and give a brief explanation of each:

Category	Explanation

2 List the main effects of abuse on children:

....

....

....

....

3 List any factors that may increase the likelihood of risk:

....

....

....

....

See page 92 for activity feedback.

2.6 Identifying Signs of Abuse

Recognising abuse is not easy, even for individuals who are experienced in working with abuse. Often personal feelings of shock or anger can interfere with the recognition that abuse is, or may be, taking place, and it is easy to deny that it is happening. This section is not designed to make you an expert, but to make you more alert to the signs of possible abuse in all five areas. By the end, you should be able to identify the possible signs and indicators of each type of abuse – neglect, physical, sexual, emotional and bullying or harassment. Start by tackling the next activity.

© Alan Spink

ACTIVITY 19

Jot down any signs or indicators that would make you concerned that a child is being abused. An example has been given to start you off.

Example
Unexplained injuries or bruising.

....

....

....

....

....

....

....

....

....

....

....

....

....

....

....

....

See page 93 for activity feedback.

Neglect

Because neglect is where adults consistently or regularly fail to meet a child's basic physical and/or psychological needs, it is likely to result in the serious impairment of the child's health or development. It can go unnoticed for a long time, yet have lasting and very damaging effects on children. Children who do not receive adequate food or physical care will often develop and mature more slowly, while those who are left alone, unsupervised or unoccupied, will often find it difficult to make friends or socialise adequately. It is important to be able to recognise both physical and emotional indicators.

Remember!

Physical indicators of neglect include:

- constant hunger, sometimes begging or stealing food from other children

- an unkempt state (frequently dirty or smelly)

- loss of weight or being constantly underweight

- inappropriate dress.

Behavioural indicators of neglect include:

- being tired all the time

- frequently being late for school or not going to school at all

- failing to attend hospital or medical appointments

- having few friends

- being left alone or unsupervised on a regular basis.

© Alan Edwards

ACTIVITY 20

Read John's story, then answer the questions provided.

John is 14 years of age and uses a wheelchair. He is cared for by his dad, as his mum died over a year ago. He has been learning basketball over the past three years and is delighted to have been chosen to participate in an international tour in six months' time. This clearly involves a good deal of planning and a number of meetings.

John does not attend the first two meetings. He says his dad is unable to bring him. For the second two meetings, John asks if you would collect and return him home in the evenings at about 10pm. You agree this with his dad and let other coaches in your club know about the arrangement. In this case, it is difficult to say no to requests for transport, even though you are not really comfortable with the situation, so you arrange for another coach to accompany you and John. On both occasions, there is no one at home when you return John, and the house is cold and dark. John has not eaten since lunchtime. You offer to make John a cup of tea and, on going to the cupboard, find there is very little food. John does not know where his dad is; he seems to accept the fact that he may not return until much later and says he is quite often left alone, sometimes all night. John doesn't seem to mind, for he says he can get himself to bed and his dad is usually there in the mornings.

1   As John feels quite happy about his dad not being there, do you feel it is acceptable for him to be alone?

....

....

....

....

....

2   What do you think you might do in this situation?

....

....

....

....

....

See page 93 for activity feedback.

Physical Abuse

Most children will collect cuts and bruises in their daily life, and certainly through their involvement in sport.

ACTIVITY 21

1   Jot down the typical soft tissue injuries likely to be sustained in your sport.

....

....

....

....

....

....

....

2   Note any areas where you might expect abrasions and bruising from participation in your sport.

....

....

....

....

....

....

....

See page 94 for activity feedback.

ACTIVITY 22

Read Mary's story, then answer the questions below.

Mary Carter is six years of age. She has come to swimming lessons during the summer holidays with her elder brother Peter, who is 10. Mary and Peter's family is well known in the local area; their father is a bank manager at the local branch and their mother is a senior manager at a local computer company. Mary's mother, Pamela, works long hours and is often away on business. However, Mary and Peter are normally happy, lively and outgoing children.

Yesterday, Mrs Carter came to collect Mary and Peter from the leisure centre but was clearly in a rush. Mary had not finished changing and Mrs Carter bundled her roughly out of the centre into the car. Today, Mary arrives at the pool in a distressed state. During the lesson, Catherine, Mary's coach, notices that she has five straight red marks on the back of her thigh.

1   Do you think Catherine should be concerned about Mary? If so, why?

....

....

....

....

2   What do you think are the causes of the marks on Mary's leg?

....

....

....

....

3   Are there any other concerns you have about this situation?

....

....

....

....

See page 95 for activity feedback.

ACTIVITY 23

53

Jot down any other form of potential physical abuse that occurs or may occur in your sport:

....

....

....

....

....

....

....

....

....

....

....

....

....

....

....

....

....

....

See page 95 for activity feedback.

Sexual Abuse

How will you know if a child is being sexually abused? Because physical signs are difficult to observe on a day-to-day, routine basis, a child's behaviour may be the only outward indicator of sexual abuse. Often concerns will be reported to you by a third party (eg a friend of the child, or another adult who has heard or noticed something that gives rise for concern).

Children may tell you either directly or indirectly that they are being sexually abused. Direct disclosures from children are comparatively rare. This will have taken enormous courage on their part because it is likely that they will feel ashamed and will have been threatened by the abuser about what will happen if they tell, and/or will be aware and very frightened of the potential consequences (eg the abuser going to prison). In all cases, children will tell you because they want the abuse to stop. Therefore, it is very important that you listen to them and take them seriously.

Remember!

There may be **physical indicators** of sexual abuse, such as:

- pain or itching in the genital area
- bruising or bleeding near the genital area
- having a sexually transmitted disease
- vaginal discharge or infection
- stomach pains
- discomfort when walking or sitting down
- pregnancy.

If you suspect or become aware of such indicators, it is inappropriate for you to check them out yourself. In these circumstances, always refer the child to a medical expert and discuss your concerns with your club/organisation welfare or child protection officer.

The sort of **behavioural indicators** you may notice include:

- sudden or unexplained changes in behaviour (eg becoming aggressive or withdrawn)
- apparent fear of someone
- running away from home
- having nightmares
- having sexual knowledge that is beyond the child's age or developmental level
- making sexual drawings or using sexual language
- wetting the bed
- having eating problems, such as overeating or anorexia
- self-harming or mutilating, sometimes leading to suicide attempts
- saying they have secrets they cannot tell anyone about
- abusing substances or drugs
- suddenly having unexplained sources of money
- taking over a parental role at home and seeming beyond their age level
- not being allowed to have friends (particularly in adolescence)
- acting in a sexually explicit way towards adults
- a child telling someone about the abuse.

ACTIVITY 24

Read the following story, then answer the questions below.

Carole is a young woman, aged 14. She has learning difficulties, a developmental level of about 11 years and is partially hearing impaired, although she can lip-read. Carole is participating in outdoor activities as part of her school's curriculum. This means that she attends the outdoor centre every Wednesday afternoon. One afternoon there is an indoor lesson, covering the basic skills required for orienteering. During some individual time with Carole, she tells you that she does not like Tony, her mum's boyfriend. She does not say any more than this but later has a sudden outburst of temper, which is unusual. When Carole calms down it is nearly time to go home, although she seems very reluctant to go.

1   Would you start to have some concerns about Carole? If so, what would they be?

....

....

....

....

....

....

....

2   What do you think you might do at this stage?

....

....

....

....

....

....

See page 95 for activity feedback.

Emotional Abuse

Emotional abuse is perhaps the most difficult of all forms of abuse to measure. Often, children who appear well cared for may be emotionally abused by being taunted, put down or belittled, or because they receive little or no love, affection or attention from their parents or carers. Coaches and others involved in performance sport should also consider the potential emotional abuse from excessive pressure during training regimes or in relation to competition.

Remember!

Physical indicators of emotional abuse may include:

- a failure to thrive or grow, particularly if the child puts on weight in other circumstances (eg in hospital or away from home)
- sudden speech disorders
- developmental delay, either in terms of physical or emotional progress.

Behavioural indicators may include:

- neurotic behaviour (eg hair twisting, rocking)
- being unable to play, unwilling to take part
- excessive fear of making mistakes
- sudden speech disorders
- self-harm or mutilation
- fear of parents being contacted.

© Alan Edwards

ACTIVITY 25

Read the following story, then answer the questions below.

Kea is 12 years old. She is Japanese and came to live in England with her parents two years ago. She is an excellent gymnast and a regular attendee at her local club. Both Kea's parents are supportive and encourage her gymnastics.

You are one of the coaches at the gymnastics club. Tom, one of your colleagues, usually coaches Kea. You have known Tom for years. He has a reputation for being one of the lads, and is always joking and teasing the young gymnasts, particularly the young women. Although you feel uncomfortable about this, the younger gymnasts seem eager to please Tom to gain his praise.

One Saturday morning, you notice that during a gymnastics exercise, Tom puts his arm around Kea's shoulders and then pats her bottom as she goes away. She makes a mistake during the exercise and Tom makes what you consider to be a racist comment. Later in the day, you hear him shouting at Kea, telling her she is rubbish and that there is no hope for her. Kea is clearly distressed by this but he ignores her. This is not the first time you have had concerns about Tom and you decide to challenge his behaviour. He puts you down, says you cannot take a joke, and claims Kea enjoys all the attention.

1   What feelings does this raise for you?

. . . .

. . . .

. . . .

2   Do you have concerns about the way Tom is behaving? If so, why?

. . . .

. . . .

. . . .

3   What action do you think you might take?

. . . .

. . . .

. . . .

See page 96 for activity feedback.

Bullying and Harassment

The damage inflicted by bullying and harassment is frequently underestimated. It can cause considerable distress to children, to the extent that it affects their health and development or, in extreme cases, causes them significant harm (including self-harm). There are a number of signs that may indicate that a child is being bullied; these are outlined below.

Remember!

Physical indicators may include:

- stomach aches or headaches
- difficulty in sleeping
- bed-wetting
- scratches or bruising
- damaged clothes
- bingeing (eg on food, cigarettes or alcohol)
- a shortage of money
- frequent loss of possessions.

Behavioural indicators may include:

- fear and/or avoidance of a particular individual or group
- reduced concentration
- becoming withdrawn or depressed
- being clingy
- emotional fluctuations or mood swings (eg tearful)
- a reluctance to go to school/training
- a drop in performance in sport or at school.

2.7 Summary

In this section, you have had the chance to consider your own feelings about child protection issues and have been encouraged to consider specific situations. You have also been asked to consider the different categories of abuse and should now be able to relate them to your own sport.

The indicators outlined in Section 2.6 are very important but, even if children display some or all of these signs, it does not necessarily mean they are being abused. **It is not your responsibility to decide**. However, it is your responsibility to **act by reporting your concerns if you suspect abuse**.

Your observations could be the missing piece in a larger jigsaw of concerns, which is already being pieced together by child protection professionals, such as social workers and the police. This is why it is vital that you are aware of all the signs and indicators, both in terms of what you see (ie physical signs) and in what you observe (ie behavioural signs).

Child abuse, particularly sexual abuse, can arouse strong emotions in those facing such a situation. It is important to acknowledge and understand these emotions and to not allow them to interfere with your judgement about what action to take.

In the last few activities in this section, you started to think about what you might do in certain situations. Section 3 takes this a little further and considers what steps to take if you think a child is being abused.

3.0 Introduction

You should always take immediate action by reporting your concerns if a child says or indicates that he is being abused, or if you have reason to suspect that this is the case.

In this section, you will be encouraged to consider how you should respond to a child for whom you have concerns, either as a result of a disclosure from the child, your own observations or the concerns of others. You will also see that, by developing procedures to both prevent and deal with such situations, it is possible to provide both a fun and safe sporting environment for children.

By the end of this section, you should be able to:

- describe how you would respond to a child who discloses abuse

- recognise the importance of your own observations in the detection of possible abuse

- identify the person(s) to whom you should report or share your concern

- deal with difficult situations involving allegations against parents/carers or other staff/volunteers

- deal with incidents of bullying

- describe the responsibilities of various agencies/organisations, including your club/organisation, governing bodies of sport, local authorities, social services and the police

- prepare yourself for the possibility of having to deal with suspected abuse in the future.

3.1 Dealing with Disclosures of Abuse

Children who are being abused will only tell people that they trust and with whom they feel safe. Coaches very often share a close relationship with their performers and may, therefore, be the sort of person in whom a child might place her trust. Children want the abuse to stop. By listening and taking what a child is telling you seriously, you will already be helping to protect them.

It is useful to think in advance about how you might respond to this situation in such a way as to avoid putting yourself at risk. The following guidelines are included in most governing bodies of sport child protection policies and procedures, and it is strongly recommended that they are incorporated into those of your own club/organisation.

Timing and Location

Understandably, a child who has been abused may want to see you alone, away from others. She may, therefore, approach you at the end of a session when everyone is going home, or may arrive deliberately early at a time when she thinks you will not be busy. However, a disclosure is not just a quick chat, it will take time and usually has further consequences. Bear in mind that you may also need to attend to other children, check equipment or set up an activity – you cannot simply leave a session unattended. Therefore, try to arrange to speak to the child at an appropriate time.

Location is very important. Although it is important to respect the child's need for privacy, you also need to protect yourself against misinterpretation or potential allegations. Do not listen to the child's disclosure in a completely private place – try to ensure that other members of staff are present or at least nearby.

Responding to the Child

It will have taken a great deal of courage for a child to tell you about abusive behaviour and it is crucial that you take this into consideration when responding to the child's disclosure. Following the guidance in the box below will help you to act in an appropriate and responsible manner.

Guidance in Responding to a Child

- Do not panic – react calmly, so as not to frighten the child.

- Acknowledge that what the child is doing is difficult, but that they are right to confide in you.

- Reassure the child that they are not to blame.

- Make sure that, from the outset, you can understand what the child is saying.

- Be honest straight away and tell the child you cannot make promises that you will not be able to keep.

- Do not promise that you will keep the conversation a secret. Explain that in order to help them you will need to involve other people and that you will need to write things down.

- Listen carefully to the child; take them seriously.

- Do not allow your shock or distaste to show.

- Keep any questions to the minimum required for you to clarify any facts or words that you do not understand – do not speculate or make assumptions.

- Do not probe for more information than is offered.

- Encourage the child to use their own words.

- Do not make negative comments about the alleged abuser.

- At the end of the conversation, ensure that the child is either being collected or is capable of going home on their own.

- Do not approach the alleged abuser.

Recording the Disclosure

Once the child has left, make an accurate written record of what was said. You should use your governing body/club/organisation's standard incident report form, or the sample form on the following page as a template.

Once you have completed the written record:

- sign and date it

- provide your club welfare officer and others with copies, as required by your club/organisation's child protection procedures

- store the information in accordance with your club/organisation or governing body of sport procedures (as a minimum, somewhere safe and secure).

Other Sources of Concern – reports, allegations or suspicions of abuse

In addition to a child making a direct disclosure of abuse to you, concerns may arise in a number of other ways. These include:

- a conversation with an adult (eg another parent, spectator or colleague) or another child

- direct observation of a worrying incident

- observation of signs, indicators or behaviour that suggest possible abuse

- receipt of an anonymous allegation (eg by phone, text, email or letter).

These should be recorded in the same way as disclosures, using an incident report form.

Child Protection Incident Report Form

Child's name: .... Date of Birth: ....

Address: ....

....

.... Postcode: ....

Disability: .... Ethnicity: ....

Home/parent's telephone number: ....

Sports club/school child attends: ....

Date of incident/report/disclosure: ....

Time: .... Venue: ....

If concerns were passed on by a third party, supply their details (name, contact number etc), and record what was said:

....

(continue overleaf if necessary)

If the child/young person made a direct disclosure, describe the circumstances and record what the child said (using their words): ....

....

(continue overleaf if necessary)

If concerns arise from your observations/actions, give details: ....

....

Name, role, relationship to the child, and contact details (if known) of any alleged perpetrator(s):

....

Name, role and contact details of any potential witnesses to the alleged incident:

....

Any actions that you have taken (include name, role, agency and contact number for person(s) with whom this information has been shared, including parents, and any agreed actions):

Your name: .... Role: ....

Contact no: ....

Signature: ....

Pass this form on to .... in line with your club/organisation's procedures.

Please ensure confidentiality and share your concerns on a strict need-to-know basis, and only in order to protect this child or other children.

You may wish to seek reassurance by discussing your concerns with someone outside the club/organisation.

The NSPCC Helpline provides a free, 24-hour service on **0808-800 5000**.

Dealing with Bullying

All incidents or suspicions of bullying must be taken very seriously. The guidelines in the box below will help your club/organisation deal with the issue appropriately:

How to Deal with Bullying

- Develop guidelines on dealing with bullying and ensure that these are part of an active policy.

- Promote the guidelines in your club/organisation's code of practice.

- Ensure that the concepts of equity, value and inclusion are covered in staff training.

- Take all signs of bullying seriously.

- Involve parents and carers.

- Do not ignore the victim or the bully – encourage them to discuss their thoughts both with you and, if appropriate, with others within the group.

- Encourage the children involved to change their behaviour in order to improve the situation.

- Follow general guidelines – listen, record, report, reassure and take appropriate action.

- Invite professional organisations to explain specific issues to children and offer further help – this could be a session for both coaches and children.

- Share concerns – the victim may not be safe.

- Follow up what you do – remember that sport should be safe and fun for both the bully and the victim.

- If the bullying incident was severe in nature (eg a serious assault), or bullying behaviour persists despite attempts to deal with it, this should be reported and dealt with in line with the club/organisation's child protection policy and procedures (including consideration of the need to refer the matter to statutory services).

3.2 Responding to Observations

Children

Due to the nature of coaching, you have a unique opportunity to observe children both physically and emotionally. For example, it is now quite common for coaches to carry out a fitness assessment prior to the start of a coaching programme, during which personal details are recorded (eg height, weight and body measurements). These can prove useful if a child shows signs of rapid change through diet or weight training. However, always remember to obtain the parents' or carers' consent to collect this kind of information when a child joins your club/organisation.

Colleagues

Remember, you not only have to consider the consequences of your own actions, but also those of others within your club/organisation. For example, from time to time, you may be required to observe other coaches' sessions and may have concerns or spot risks that, for whatever reason, have been missed by the coach leading the session. In these circumstances, you may need to intervene, either by stopping the session or simply discussing your concerns with the coach in question. This should be viewed as good practice, rather than interfering, as failure to take action could result in a case of negligence being made against the coach and/or club. The incident should be recorded in writing and made available to other coaches to avoid them making the same mistake themselves.

Whereas some incidents are clearly a cause for concern and may prompt action (such as a risk assessment, change to coaching style or review of goals), be aware that some incidents are not so obvious and only surface once the damage has occurred.

3.3 Sharing Your Concerns

As a result of a disclosure or an observation, you may be worried about what a child has said or simply have a feeling that something is not quite right. Taking action in cases of child abuse is never easy and you will inevitably experience a mixture of emotions. You may feel that you have been partly responsible; you may be worried about the consequences of the action you take for the child's family or others. These feelings are completely natural, particularly because of the nature of the media's coverage of child abuse.

What is important is the child's long-term future – imagine what could happen if you do not take action. Sadly, in some extreme cases, a failure to act has led to a child's death, as many child abuse inquiries have shown. At the very least, a failure to act may well result in the continuing abuse of one or more children. Your information could be vital in preventing further abuse and you have a responsibility to share and/or report your concerns, however small they may be. Many adult survivors of childhood abuse have said that telling someone who helped stop the abuse was a vital step in the healing process.

Sharing with a Designated Person, Welfare Officer or Senior Colleague

In some sport situations, it may be quite easy to determine who you should contact if you are concerned about a child being abused. For example, if you work for a local authority, in a sport or leisure centre, or at a school, there should be staff with designated child protection responsibilities. If not, you will have a senior colleague or line manager (the person to whom you are directly responsible/your employer/the person who appointed you) to contact. If your work with children takes place at a sports club, your governing body of sport is likely to have a lead child protection officer, and your club should have a club welfare officer, to whom you can report your concerns. Failing this, you should speak to the club secretary or chairperson. Whether you are a paid employee or volunteer, there should be someone to whom you can turn.

However, in some circumstances, particularly if you work in a voluntary capacity, there may be no obvious person to whom you can report any concerns you may have. For example, you may coach at a club operating after

school or for a local team on a Saturday morning. In this case, it is particularly important to plan what you would do if you suspected abuse, before you are actually faced with a real-life situation.

> **Remember!**
>
> Whoever you talk to, you will need to maintain confidentiality, but do not need to take full responsibility. Your lead child protection officer, club welfare officer or senior colleague will expect to be informed so that you can begin to protect the child and be supported in what could be a difficult situation.

Sharing with Parents/Carers

You should always be committed to working in partnership with parents or carers when there are concerns about their children. In most situations, it is therefore important to talk to parents or carers to help clarify any initial concerns. In doing so, you may discover reasons that explain behavioural changes or find out that the family needs further support. Parents and carers will usually inform someone at your club/organisation if their child is upset or unwell, but occasionally this information may not reach you. In cases like this, simply talking to parents or carers can help to resolve any initial concerns.

If the concerns are about someone who also plays a role within sport, then the club welfare officer or a senior colleague should inform the relevant sporting organisation's lead child protection officer, in line with agreed procedures.

Sharing with Professionals

In some situations, particularly if it would be inappropriate to discuss your concerns with the child's parents or carers,[16] it may be necessary to inform social services and/or the police. If available, your organisational lead child protection officer, club welfare officer or senior colleague/line manager should take responsibility for this. However, you need to be aware of what to do in case she is unavailable or inappropriate (eg the concerns relate to this person), or there is no one obvious to whom to report your concerns. The process is as follows:

---

[16] See pages 64–65 for further details.

1 Inform the duty officer at social services or the police and explain that your referral involves child protection. Give your name, role, address and telephone number (this is helpful rather than required). Give clear, accurate details of the child (ie name, address and date of birth), what you have observed (include date and time, details of the child's behaviour and emotional state), what the child has said and what action you have taken. This is the type of information you should have recorded on the incident report form (your club/organisation /governing body of sport or the sample form on page 61).

2 Social services/police will advise you on what to do next, including whether, how and when to involve parents/carers, and will also take responsibility for ensuring that appropriate enquiries and investigations are undertaken.

3 If a child needs urgent medical attention as a result of suspected abuse, then you must seek this as a matter of urgency. Inform medical staff of your suspicions of possible abuse and contact social services as soon as possible to obtain advice about involving parents.

4 Record carefully what you have heard, seen and done, including conversations you have had with other professionals, using the appropriate incident report form (see point 1 above).

3.4 Dealing with Difficult Situations

Allegations Against Parents/Carers

In some cases, a child may be placed at even greater risk if you share your concerns with his parents or carers (eg when a parent or carer may be responsible for the abuse, or is not able to respond to the situation appropriately). In these circumstances, you must report any suspicion, allegation or incident of abuse to the relevant child protection or welfare officer as soon as possible and ensure that it is recorded in writing. If this person is not available, refer your concerns to social services or the police immediately.

Remember!

- Maintain confidentiality on a need-to-know basis only.

- Ensure the relevant child protection or welfare officer follows up with social services.

- The child protection or welfare officer should seek advice from social services about whether, when and how to consult the child's parents or carers.

Remember!

- However small your concern, share it with the club welfare officer, organisational lead child protection officer or senior colleague/line manager, who will take responsibility for deciding whether to inform social services. If no one is available (or your concern is about this person), then you must ring social services yourself, giving accurate details of your concerns.

- Social services departments have a responsibility to investigate all concerns of child abuse[17]; they do this jointly with the police[18]. This may involve talking to the child and their family and/or gathering more information.

- It is important to be open and honest with parents, but in some circumstances this may put the child in more danger. If in doubt, discuss your concerns first with appropriate and qualified personnel.

[17] See pages 68–69 for further details.
[18] See pages 68–69 for further details.

Allegations Against Staff/Volunteers

As a coach, you are responsible for the welfare of each child in your care, and for making others aware of their own responsibilities (eg volunteers helping out with trips, tours or social events). However, child abuse can and does occur outside the family setting, and it also sometimes occurs in sport.

Hearing allegations of child abuse against coaches, members of staff or volunteers is particularly distressing. It can raise feelings of anger because the children have placed their trust in adults who have abused that trust, and guilt on the part of other colleagues, who may feel they could have done more to stop it happening. An immediate response is to want to deny the possibility that the allegation could be true. Reporting suspicions, allegations or incidents of abuse against a colleague can be equally distressing. Clubs/organisations should assure all coaches, staff and volunteers that they will fully

support and protect anyone who, in good faith, reports his concern about a colleague's practice or the possibility that a child is being abused.

The diagram on the next page outlines the action you should take if you are concerned about the behaviour of a member of staff or volunteer in your club/organisation. The same procedure applies in all cases, even if allegations are made some time after the event (eg by an adult who was abused as a child by a member of staff who is still working with children).

> **Remember!**
>
> The child will and should be at the centre of the whole process; their confidence, safety and security must be assured

© Alan Edwards

The diagram below offers some general guidelines on how to respond to any concerns you may have about staff or volunteers in your club/organisation. However, these guidelines are by no means definitive – you should also refer to your club/organisation's policy.

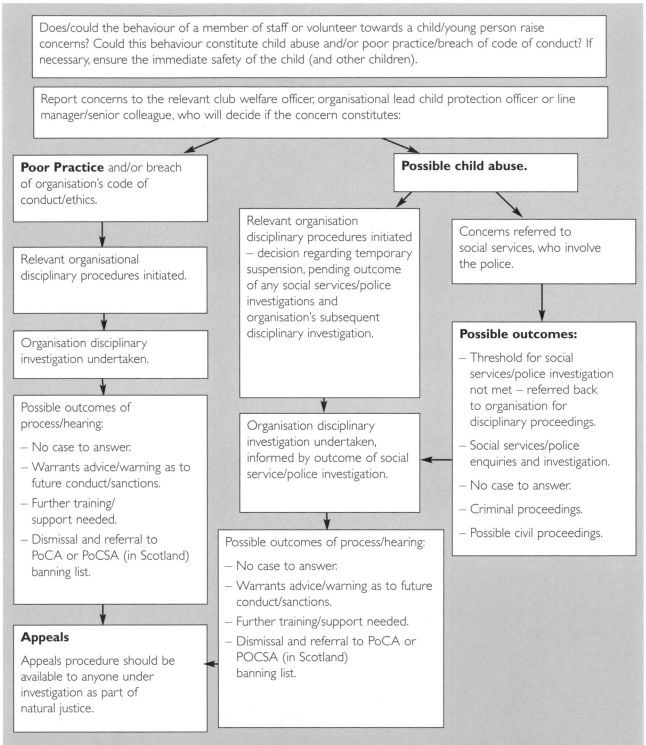

Does/could the behaviour of a member of staff or volunteer towards a child/young person raise concerns? Could this behaviour constitute child abuse and/or poor practice/breach of code of conduct? If necessary, ensure the immediate safety of the child (and other children).

Report concerns to the relevant club welfare officer, organisational lead child protection officer or line manager/senior colleague, who will decide if the concern constitutes:

Poor Practice and/or breach of organisation's code of conduct/ethics.

Possible child abuse.

Relevant organisational disciplinary procedures initiated.

Relevant organisation disciplinary procedures initiated – decision regarding temporary suspension, pending outcome of any social services/police investigations and organisation's subsequent disciplinary investigation.

Concerns referred to social services, who involve the police.

Organisation disciplinary investigation undertaken.

Possible outcomes of process/hearing:

– No case to answer.

– Warrants advice/warning as to future conduct/sanctions.

– Further training/ support needed.

– Dismissal and referral to PoCA or PoCSA (in Scotland) banning list.

Organisation disciplinary investigation undertaken, informed by outcome of social service/police investigation.

Possible outcomes:

– Threshold for social services/police investigation not met – referred back to organisation for disciplinary proceedings.

– Social services/police enquiries and investigation.

– No case to answer.

– Criminal proceedings.

– Possible civil proceedings.

Possible outcomes of process/hearing:

– No case to answer.

– Warrants advice/warning as to future conduct/sanctions.

– Further training/support needed.

– Dismissal and referral to PoCA or POCSA (in Scotland) banning list.

Appeals

Appeals procedure should be available to anyone under investigation as part of natural justice.

If you do not know who to turn to for advice or are worried about sharing your concerns with someone inside your club or organisation, contact social services directly (or the NSPCC Child Protection Helpline on 0808-800 5000 or Childline on 0800-1111).

Figure 2: Responding to concerns about staff/volunteers

Allegations of abuse against members of staff in any setting can have far-reaching consequences. Other children, parents and members of staff may need to be interviewed by the police and social services. The effects on other staff can be distressing, and child protection policies and recruitment/selection procedures may need to be reviewed.

There may be three types of investigation:

- Criminal   (police)
- Child protection   (social services/police)
- Disciplinary   (employing/
                                deploying organisation)

Civil proceedings may also be initiated by the alleged victim, their family, or the person accused.

The club/organisation's designated child protection officer (if available) should make his governing body of sport equivalent aware of the allegation and seek advice as appropriate (eg how to deal with the media). However, if the club/organisation's child protection officer is the subject of the allegation, a senior person from the club/organisation should report directly to the governing body of sport's lead child protection officer.

The club/organisation and/or governing body of sport should make an immediate decision about whether an individual accused of abuse should be temporarily suspended from coaching pending further police and social services inquiries.

Irrespective of the findings of social services or police inquiries, the club/organisation must assess all available information in each case, under the appropriate misconduct/disciplinary procedure, to decide whether the accused should be reinstated and, if so, how this can be handled sensitively with other staff or volunteers. The welfare of children should always be the primary consideration, even when there is insufficient evidence either to take the matter to court, or to secure a conviction. It is important to note that the burden of proof required to secure a conviction is 'beyond reasonable doubt'. This is a higher threshold than that required in child protection/welfare proceedings (including sport organisations' disciplinary and misconduct procedures), where a judgement is made 'on the balance of probability' about whether allegations are true and an individual is a potential risk to children.

3.5 Responsibilities of Agencies/Organisations

Remember!

If you suspect that a child may be being abused, it is not your responsibility to take control of the situation, nor to decide whether or not child abuse is actually taking place. However, you do have a responsibility to report your concerns and to ensure the safety of the children under your supervision. You should therefore use your club/organisation's reporting procedures to inform the appropriate agencies/organisation of your concerns, so that they can make enquiries and take any action that may be necessary to protect the child.

Your Club/Organisation

The last thing you should have to do when an incident of child abuse is suspected, is to search through the telephone directory to find out who to contact. Your role at this time will be to respond calmly and appropriately (you may need to reassure the child if a direct disclosure has been made) – not to appear confused or unsure of what to do. Your club/organisation should therefore have a child protection policy and procedures document that explains the process to follow.

In addition, your club/organisation should identify a designated person to handle child protection issues. This person should complete a self-declaration form and undergo a criminal records check for quality assurance purposes. The designated person will require support from your club and/or the wider organisation and appropriate training. This support should be provided as part of the child protection policy and implementation procedures adopted by your club/organisation.

Processes and procedures are never solutions in themselves, but should always be adopted as a means of ensuring better outcomes for the children involved. No guidance can, or should, attempt to offer a detailed prescription of how to work with each individual child or family. Good practice calls for the effective cooperation between different agencies and professions.

Governing Bodies of Sport

In recent years, governing bodies of sport have recognised the need to:

- publish child protection policies, procedures and codes of ethics and conduct

- address sensitive areas, such as manual handling during training sessions on the delivery of their sports

- support and protect coaches and provide advice in areas such as recruitment, insurance, first aid and resource use.

All governing bodies of sport are now required to have child protection policies and implementation plans, and should also have appointed a lead officer in child protection. Increasingly, governing bodies of sport have established systems to facilitate criminal records checking of coaches and others who come into contact with children, and case referral/management groups to ensure that reported concerns are managed appropriately.

Local Authorities

In order to fulfil their social service responsibilities, local authorities have specific legal duties in respect of the Children Act 1989 and 2004, the Protection of Children Act 1999, the Children (NI) Order 1995 and the Children (Scotland) Act 1995. Each local authority should work to safeguard the welfare of children in partnership with other public agencies, the voluntary sector and service users and carers. Local authorities have the lead responsibility to provide effective services for children in need. In England and Wales, local safeguarding children boards (LSCBs) replaced area child protection committees in 2006.

Local authorities are often involved in play-/activity-scheme provision. You may be coaching or working in a play/activity scheme, either during a school holiday or for a specific programme. Many local authorities will provide the expertise of a community sports coordinator to make sure that all those involved in such coaching activities have access to the most appropriate resources, including coach education.

Detailed safeguarding and child protection policies and procedures should also be produced by all local authorities. They should provide guidance on all aspects of good practice and child protection for coaches, staff and volunteers.

Social Services and Children's Social Care

Following changes introduced within the Children Act 2004, in England social services have become part of wider local authority children and families services that also incorporate education services. Titles for these services and staff roles within them vary widely, although the government has introduced the term 'children's social care' for these new, combined departments.

Social services (or their new equivalent) provide a wide range of care and support for adults, children and families. This includes older people; people with physical or learning disabilities; people with mental health or substance misuse problems; ex-offenders and young offenders; families, especially where children have special needs; children at risk of harm; children who need to be accommodated or looked after by the local authority through fostering or residential care; children who are placed for adoption.

Social services have a statutory duty under the Children Act 1989 and 2004, the Protection of Children Act 1999, the Children (NI) Order 1995 and the Children (Scotland) Act 1995, to ensure the welfare of children. In England and Wales, this includes working with LSCBs and, in Scotland, with the local child protection committee, to comply with its procedures for responding to and managing child protection referrals and cases. When a child protection referral is made, social services have a legal responsibility to make enquiries and investigate if they have reason to suspect that a child in their area is suffering, or is likely to suffer, significant harm.

A child who is at risk of significant harm will invariably be a child in need. Social services are responsible for coordinating an assessment of the:

- child's needs

- parents' capacity to keep the child safe

- parents' capacity to promote the child's welfare

- wider family circumstances.

This assessment will involve sharing information with the police and significant others (eg health or education authorities). In some cases, this may include information from a sports club/organisation or members of its staff. Where the child is thought to be in immediate danger, social services may apply to the courts for emergency powers to ensure a child's safety by placing the child under the protection of the local authority.

Because of their responsibilities, duties and powers in relation to vulnerable children, social services act as the principle point of contact for children if there are child welfare concerns. They may also be contacted directly by parents, family members seeking help, concerned friends and neighbours and professionals, or others from statutory and voluntary agencies.

Police

The police have two primary duties: to protect life and limb and to investigate crime. Within this, they recognise the fundamental importance of inter-agency working in combating child abuse. All forces have child protection units and, despite variations in their structure, they will normally take primary responsibility for investigating child abuse cases. They also have emergency powers to enter premises and ensure the immediate protection of children believed to be suffering from, or at risk of, significant harm. At the conclusion of their investigation, the police will pass their file to the Crown Prosecution Service (CPS) in England and Wales, the Public Prosecution Service (PPS) in Northern Ireland or the Procurator Fiscal Service (PF) in Scotland to determine whether criminal proceedings should be initiated.

Other Agencies/Organisations

A number of additional agencies/organisations can provide important routes for children in need to enter into statutory and voluntary services – these include:

- ChildLine[19]
- NSPCC Child Protection Helplines[20]
- Scottish Children's Reporter Administration (SCRA)[21]
- education services
- cultural and leisure services
- health services
- day-care services
- probation services
- prison service
- youth justice services
- voluntary and private sectors.

There may also be local support groups in your area that you could approach for guidance, support or practical help.

---

[19] ChildLine is available for all children in trouble or in danger (Tel: 0800-1111).

[20] The NSPCC Child Protection Helpline offers confidential advice to children, young people and adults with concerns (Tel: 0808-800 5000). The NSPCC also provide a text phone service (Tel: 0800-056 0566) and an online service for children and young people (www.achancetotalk.com).

[21] The Children's Hearings System is unique to Scotland and was established in 1971 to address the needs and behaviour of children and young people who face serious problems in their lives. These problems can include, for example, a child committing an offence, the child's parents having difficulty looking after them or a child failing to attend school. For more information, visit www.scra.gov.uk

3.6 Taking Preparatory Action

It is important to be prepared for the possibility of having to deal with suspected abuse in the future, so that, in the event, you are able to respond calmly and appropriately.

The following action points relate to your club/organisation's records and are things you should be able to tackle more or less immediately:

- Children's names:
  - Check that names are complete and spelt correctly.

- Be aware that parents/carers' surnames may be different from that of the children.
- Phone numbers:
  - Check that numbers are up to date and include area codes.
  - Check that mobile numbers are correct.
- Addresses:
  - Check that addresses are complete and up to date.
  - If possible, obtain a map of the local area – it is surprising how many people are unfamiliar with it.

ACTIVITY 26

Jot down in the space provided below any additional action points that you think would help you:

....

....

....

....

....

....

....

....

....

....

....

....

....

The following activity will help you compile a list of people to contact in relation to child protection issues. Take a photocopy of your completed list and keep it somewhere safe for future reference.

ACTIVITY 27

Find out the names and telephone numbers of the main child protection contacts within your club/organisation and/or governing body of sport, social services and police service, and record the details below.

Child Protection Contacts

Name of the person in your normal coaching environment to whom you should report any concerns about child protection issues: ....

Job title: ....

Address: ....

....

....Tel: ....

Club Welfare/Child Protection Officer
(if different from above): ....

Tel: ....

Organisational Lead Child Protection Officer: ....

Tel: ....

Social Services Contact: ....

Tel: ....

Police Station Contact: ....

Tel: ....

Name of local hospital: ....

Tel: ....

See page 97 for activity feedback.

What Would You Do?

In the following activities, you will be asked to consider a series of case studies and scenarios. In some cases, you will be asked to comment on the actions of the people involved; in others, you will be asked to think about how you would respond if you were involved. Remember that making the correct decision is not always straightforward. Refer to the information in this pack or contact more experienced professionals for advice and guidance.

ACTIVITY 28

Case Study 1

The following case study has been written from a parent or carer's point of view. As you read through it, jot down your concerns as a coach in the space provided.

Your children want to attend a sports team practice in your local park every Saturday morning. You agree that they can go and provide them with some money, sports kits and drinks. As the park is not far away and near to their school, you agree that they can walk there together, unaccompanied, and feel assured that they will be safe. The practice goes well; the children seem keen and the session is popular, with lots of other children and parents attending.

After a while, the enthusiastic coaches enter a local tournament. As a result of this, even more children turn up to practices, several teams are formed and a request is made to parents to provide a donation in order to buy equipment. You decide to go and watch a practice – you have not really thought to do so in the past and wish to see the set-up. However, you do not tell your children that you intend to turn up. On arriving at the park, you are disturbed to see lots of children playing sport, but no sign of your own. You spot an adult, but he is just another parent having a game. You begin to get very concerned and quite worried – it is time for the practice to end and still there is no sign of your children.

More parents gather and you learn that some of the children have been taken to play a match across the other side of town – in cars by other parents. You also learn that your children are in this team. Time passes very slowly. It is cold and you do not really know what to do; it begins to rain and there is no shelter. You have just about had enough, when out of a car step your children, who happily tell you that they won their match in extra time.

You are introduced to the coaches who turn out to be teenagers – they are in the sixth form at school and just love playing sport.

Your concerns:

....

....

....

....

....

....

Case Study 2

Now compare Case Study 1 with the following, which has also been written from a parent or carer's perspective. As you read through it, jot down any examples of good practice that you come across in the space provided.

Your children want to take up sport on a Saturday morning. You are pleased because there is a well-established local club nearby. You telephone the organiser who sends you an information pack about the club, in which you are surprised, but pleased, to find several consent forms, a request for information about your children and a statement which sets out the club objectives and code of practice for the coaches. You are asked to complete the documentation and are invited to take your children for a trial visit.

The following Saturday, you take the children to the club to meet a coach and receive an induction to the centre. You are all very impressed with what you see and are informed that recent Lottery money has enabled the club to invest in coach training, resources and facilities. The club has been awarded Clubmark status. You are also told that, as members, you will have to be involved with the progress of your children and may be asked to contribute to some activities (eg supervising changing rooms, preparing refreshments, joining the club committee, being available for matches, fundraising events and socials).

As you tour the club, you see that some of the younger coaches are working with more experienced ones and are impressed to learn that the club employs qualified staff and makes use of volunteers. The session ends and you see that all the children are collected by their parents. They appear pleased with the morning's training and are able to speak freely to staff. Both you and your children confirm that you wish to join the club.

Examples of good practice:

....

....

....

....

....

....

....

....

....

....

....

See page 97 for activity feedback.

ACTIVITY 29

This activity is designed to help you check your understanding of good practice and the need for procedures. As you read through the following scenario, jot down any examples of good practice that you come across in the left-hand column of the table below. Then jot down any additional areas of good practice that you think should be adopted in the right-hand column.

A number of improvements have been made to Parkgate Sports Club over the past few months. These include the installation of a free drinking-water fountain, a telephone from which club members can make free local calls, security lighting and the services of a night security agency.

As the manager of a local voluntary-run club, you are responsible for recruiting staff. Your committee has approved a proposal to recruit three extra part-time leisure activity staff. You also decide to take the opportunity to recruit volunteers at the same time. You decide to place an advert in the local paper, in which you outline the aims of the club and specific areas of coaching in which you wish to recruit staff. There is an excellent response to the advert, particularly from students at a local college.

As part of your pre-recruitment checks, you send out application forms accompanied by information outlining the qualities and experience required. You also ask candidates to submit a reference. You decide to formally interview several candidates to clarify their qualifications, training needs, previous experience and expectations. At the interviews, you explain that successful candidates will be required to receive training on working with children.

You appoint three members of part-time staff and several volunteers. You explain that they will all receive an induction to the club and regular feedback on their progress.

Examples of Good Practice	Additional Recommendations

Examples of Good Practice	Additional Recommendations

See page 98 for activity feedback.

ACTIVITY 30

The following extracts are from a local sport and leisure club's records. For each one, decide what you would do if you were involved in the situation.

1   Staff complained that equipment (including trampolines, football goals and badminton posts) was not put away after being used, but just pushed into the corners of the sports hall. The storeroom in the sports hall was full of benches, chairs and cupboards.

2   One of the club's coaches raised concerns about the behaviour of a group of children attending his session. In the changing room, he discovered that shampoo had been poured into some of the children's bags, shoes had been placed in the shower and coats had been hidden in the outside bins. He was alerted to this by a parent who said that it was not the first time this had happened and that her child was unhappy and wished to leave the club. When questioned, none of the children said anything.

3   One of the senior coaches reported that he was not happy about a younger coach dating a 17-year-old performer. He knew that the relationship had been going on for some time.

4   Several children attending a sports session ending at 7.30pm were continually being left waiting by their parents until the TV soap operas finished at 8.30pm. The premises were locked at 8.00pm.

5   A member of staff asked other coaches whether they had noticed a difference in Sarah recently. At the beginning of the season, her weight had been normal for her age. However, she was now looking thin and tired, and often sat out of training sessions.

6   A fixture was abandoned due to the behaviour of the visiting team's parents on the sideline.

7   A risk assessment at the sport and leisure club revealed a substantial number of shredded cans on the grass pitches.

8   A coach noticed that one of the younger children had marks that looked like cigarette burns on his arms during an activity session in which children got hotter than usual and took their jumpers off. The child quickly covered the marks up and seemed very reluctant to discuss them.

9   A part-time coach started the season well, but soon slipped into a routine of arriving late and getting the children to set out equipment unsupervised.

10 Several parents felt uneasy about a stranger hanging around the club with a camera.

See page 98 for activity feedback.

3.7 Summary

In this section, you have been offered guidance on how to cope if you suspect a child is being abused, and on the policies and procedures your club/organisation should establish and implement in order to promote good practice and protect children.

Remember!

- The welfare of the child must be of paramount importance in all issues relating to child protection.

- Talk to parents or carers to clarify concerns about any injury or change in behaviour (unless there are indications that the parents may be responsible, sexual abuse is suspected, or the child might otherwise be placed at increased risk).

- If you are still concerned, refer to your child protection or welfare officer, or contact the duty officer at social services or the police. If a coach is involved, ensure that your sport's governing body is also informed.

- Give clear, accurate details, including the child's name and address and reasons for your concern.

- Social services will advise you about what to do next and will take responsibility for ensuring appropriate investigations are undertaken if necessary.

- If a child needs urgent medical attention as a result of suspected abuse, you must seek this as a matter of urgency, then inform social services or the police. Seek advice from social services before informing parents.

- Record carefully what you have seen, heard and done as soon as possible.

- Remember, too, that confidentiality in matters relating to child protection is vital, and information must only be shared with the child protection/welfare officer or senior colleagues (where essential) and child protection professionals.

Remember not to shoulder the burden of child protection on your own. If you are concerned or unsure, always ring social services, the police or the NSPCC. Their telephone numbers are in the local phone book. The NSPCC offers a free 24-hour national Child Protection Helpline (Tel: 0808-800 5000).

There may be issues that you need to discuss with your governing body of sport, employer or organisation – ensure that you make arrangements to meet the appropriate personnel.

If you require further information or confidential advice (for professional or personal reasons), Section 4 provides an extensive list of useful contacts and recommended further reading in relation to child protection issues.

4.0 Introduction

Part of being a good coach is being open to new ideas and training and, to some extent, being aware that you need to update your knowledge in certain areas. It is also about understanding the needs of the people you are coaching and accepting advice on how to accommodate them. If you have not already done so, you are strongly recommended to attend sports coach UK's coach workshop 'Safeguarding and Protecting Children'[22]. This section provides a comprehensive list of publications, workshops and organisations that can provide support and guidance on child protection issues.

4.1 Further Reading

This section lists a selection of useful publications and workshops that support the information provided in this pack. It is divided into subsections to make it easier to find the resource(s) you are looking for.

Sport-specific

Boocock, S. ed. (2002) 'SportsCheck: a step by step guide for sports organizations to safeguard children'. Leicester: NSPCC Child Protection in Sport Unit.

Brackenridge, C. (2001) *Spoilsports: understanding and preventing sexual exploitation in sport*. London: Routledge. ISBN: 978-0-419257-80-6.

Earle, C. (2003) *How to Coach Children in Sport*. Leeds: sports coach UK. ISBN: 978-1-902523-53-8.

Grange, J. and Gordon, R. (2001) 'SafeSport Away: a guide to good planning'. Leicester; Amateur Swimming Association and the NSPCC.

Kerr, A. (1999) *Protecting Disabled Children and Adults in Sport and Recreation: the guide*. London: Disability Sport England. ISBN: 1-902523-18-0.

McInulty, K. (2006) 'Creating a Safe Environment for Children in Sport: Scottish Governing Bodies Child Protection Guidelines' 2nd edition. Glasgow: CHILDREN 1ST.

Myers, J. and Barratt, B. (2002) 'In at the Deep End'. Leicester; NSPCC Child Protection in Sport Unit and the Amateur Swimming Association.

NSPCC Child Protection in Sport Unit (2006) 'Strategy for Safeguarding Children and Young People in Sport'. Leicester; NSPCC National Training Centre.

NSPCC Child Protection in Sport Unit (revised 2006) 'Standards for Safeguarding and Protecting Children in Sport'. Leicester: NSPCC National Training Centre.

sports coach UK (2005) *Code of Practice for Sports Coaches* (leaflet). Leeds: Coachwise Ltd.

sports coach UK (2005) *Safe and Sound* (leaflet). Leeds: Coachwise Ltd.

Sports Council for Northern Ireland (1998) 'Child Protection Fact File'. Belfast: Sports Council for Northern Ireland.

Tiivas, A. and Morton, J. (2003) 'Safe Sport Events'. Leicester: NSPCC Child Protection in Sport Unit and Sport England.

Tiivas, A. (2003) 'Time to Listen Reader'. Leicester: NSPCC Child Protection in Sport Unit.

General

Armstrong, H. (1998) *Taking Care: Church Response to Children, Adults and Abuse* London: National Children's Bureau. ISBN: 978-1-874579-85-4.

Aldgate, J., Jones, D., Rose, W. and Jeffrey, C. (eds) (2005) *The Developing World of the Child*. London: Jessica Kingsley Publishers. ISBN: 978-1-843102-44-1.

Bannister, A. (ed) (1992) *From Hearing to Healing: Working with the Aftermath of Child Sexual Abuse*. London: Longmans. ISBN: 978-0-582091-45-0.

Blagg, H., Hughes, J. A. and Wattam, C. (1989) *Child Sexual Abuse: Listening, Hearing and Validating the Experiences of Children*. London: Longmans. ISBN: 978-0-582056-47-3.

Child Care Directorate (2004) *The Protection of Children And Vulnerable Adults (NI) Order*. Belfast: DHSSPS. ISBN: 978-0-110491-25-7.

Creighton, S. (1992) *Child Abuse Trends in England and Wales, 1988–90*. London: NSPCC. ISBN: 978-0-902498-36-5.

Department of Health (2001) *Children and Young People on Child Protection Registers*. Great Britain: Department of Health. ISBN: 978-1-841824-37-6.

Department of Health, Department for Education and Skills, Home Office, Department for Culture, Media and Sports, Office of the Deputy Prime Minister and the Lord Chancellor's Department (2003). 'What to do if you're worried a child is being abused'. London: Department of Health.

---

[22] For further details, contact the sports coach UK Workshop Booking Centre (see Section 4.3 for contact details) or visit www.sportscoachuk.org

Department of Health and Children (Ireland) (2006) 'Our Duty to Care: the principles of good practice for the protection of children and young people'. Available to download from www.dohc.ie/publications/our_duty_to_care.html

DHSSNI (1995) 'The Children (NI) Order'. Northern Ireland: Department of Health and Social Services.

DHSSPS (2003) *Co-operating to Safeguard Children.* Belfast: DHSSPS. ISBN: 978-0-946932-09-2.

DHSSPS (2005) 'Area Child Protection Committee Regional Policy and Procedures 2005'. Belfast: DHSSPS

Elliot, M. (1986) *Keeping Safe: A practical guide to talking with children.* 3rd edition. London: Bedford Square Press/NCVO. ISBN: 978-0-719911-87-3.

Elliot, M. (1993) 'Protecting Children'. London: HMSO.

Glaser, D. and Frost, S. (1993) *Child Sexual Abuse.* 2nd edition. London: Macmillan. ISBN: 978-0-333576-02-1.

HMSO (1995) *Children (Northern Ireland) Order 1995.* London: HMSO. ISBN: 978-0-337370-83-0.

HMSO (2006) 'Working Together to Safeguard Children'. London: HMSO. Available to download from: www.dcsf.gov.uk/everychildmatters/resources-and-practice/IG00060/

Home Office (1993) *Safe From Harm.* London: Home Office Publications. ISBN: 978-0-862529-93-2.

Home Office (1999) 'Caring for Young People and the Vulnerable? Guidance for preventing abuse of trust'. London: Home Office.

Jones, D. and Pickett, J. (eds) (1987) *Understanding Child Abuse.* 2nd edition. London: Macmillan Educational Publications. ISBN: 978-0-333428-93-1.

Morgan, R. and Hutt, J. (2006) 'Keeping Us Safe: Report of the Safeguarding Vulnerable Children Review'. Cardiff: Welsh Assembly Government.

NSPCC (2000) *Child Maltreatment in the United Kingdom: A Study of the Prevalence of Child Abuse and Neglect.* London: NSPCC. ISBN: 978-1-842280-06-5.

The Office of the First Minister and Deputy First Minister Northern Ireland (2006) 'Our Children and Young People – Our Pledge'. Belfast: OFMDFMNI.

Scottish Executive (2002) 'It's Everyone's Job to Make Sure I'm Alright'. Edinburgh: Scottish Executive.

Scottish Executive (2003) 'Protecting Children and Young People: Framework for Standards'. Available to download from www.scotland.gov.uk/Publications/2004/03/19102/34603

Scottish Executive (2003) 'Children's Charter'. Edinburgh: Scottish Executive.

Scottish Office (1998) 'Protecting Children A Shared Responsibility – Guidance on Inter-agency Co-operation'. Edinburgh: Scottish Executive.

Stainton Rogers, W. Hevey, D. and Ash, E. (1989) *Child Abuse and Neglect: Facing the Challenge.* London: Open University Press. ISBN: 978-0-713462-16-6.

Volunteer Development Agency (2005) 'Getting It Right'. Belfast: Volunteer Development Agency.

Volunteer Development Agency (2007) 'Our Duty to Care NI'. Belfast: Volunteer Development Agency.

Wescott, H. L. (1993) *The Abuse of Children and Adults with Disabilities.* London: NSPCC. ISBN: 978-0-902498-40-2.

Welsh Assembly Government (2004) *Children and Young People: Rights to action.* Cardiff: Welsh Assembly Government. ISBN: 978-0-7504-9876-0.

Welsh Assembly Government (2009) 'Climbing Higher'. Available to download from www.sports-council-wales.org.uk/library-services.

Welsh Assembly Government (2006) *Keeping us Safe: Report of the safeguarding vulnerable children review.* Cardiff: Welsh Assembly Government. ISBN: 978-0-750440-93-6.

Welsh Assembly Government (2006) 'Report of the Safeguarding Vulnerable Children Review'. Cardiff: Welsh Assembly Government.

Welsh Assembly Government (2006) 'Safeguarding Children: Working Together under the Children Act 2004'. Cardiff: Welsh Assembly Government.

4.2 Safeguarding/Child Protection Workshops/Training

sports coach UK Workshops[23]

sports coach UK provides over 30 workshops for coaches, including:

- 'Safeguarding and Protecting Children'
- 'How to Coach Children in Sport'
- 'How to Coach Disabled People in Sport'
- 'An Introduction to Long-term Athlete Development'
- 'Coaching Children and Young People'
- 'Equity in Your Coaching'

NSPCC Child Protection in Sport Unit (CPSU) training[24]

The CPSU has developed a range of safeguarding/child protection courses and workshops, including:

- 'Safe Sports Events'
- 'Child Protection Policy and Implementation Procedures'
- 'Risk Assessment in Recruitment'
- 'Time To Listen' training for designated people (organisational leads; regional/county; and club/facility modules)

Child Protection in Sport Service (CHILDREN 1ST and sportscotland)

The following courses are available:

- 'In Safe Hands' workshop is aimed at sports club child protection officers.
- 'Supporting Clubs to Protect Children' provides training for sports development officers and active school's coordinators who support clubs in keeping children safe.

Governing Bodies of Sport Training

A number of governing bodies of sport have developed sport-specific safeguarding/child protection resources, training courses and/or workshops for coaches, staff and volunteers. Contact your governing body for further information.

County Sports Partnerships

Some county sports partnerships offer access to a number of sports coach UK workshops (as above) for local coaches and volunteers. Contact your local county sports partnership for further information.

LSCB Training

In some areas, the local safeguarding children board provides access to basic multi-agency safeguarding/child protection courses for staff/volunteers in the sports sector. Contact your local LSCB for information.

© Alan Edwards

[23] See page 82 for sports coach UK contact details.
[24] See pages 82–83 for CPSU contact details.

81

4.3 sports coach UK Contacts

sports coach UK
114 Cardigan Road
Headingley
Leeds LS6 3BJ
Tel: 0113-274 4802
Fax: 0113-275 5019
Email: coaching@sportscoachuk.org
Website: www.sportscoachuk.org

Details of all sports coach UK publications are available from:

Coachwise 1st4sport
Chelsea Close
Off Amberley Road
Armley
Leeds LS12 4HP
Tel: 0113-201 5555
Fax: 0113-231 9606
Email: enquiries@1st4sport.com
Website: www.1st4sport.com

sports coach UK works closely with governing bodies of sport and other partners to provide a comprehensive service for coaches throughout the UK. This includes an extensive programme of workshops, which have proved valuable to coaches from all types of sports and at every level of experience.

For further details of sports coach UK workshops in your area, contact:

sports coach UK Workshop Booking Centre
Tel: 0845-601 3054
Email: scukworkshop@sportscoach.org

4.4 Other Useful Contacts

This section lists a selection of organisations that can provide support and guidance on child protection issues. It is divided into subsections to make it easier to find the organisation(s) you are looking for.

Confidential Helplines

If this pack has raised personal issues for you, the following organisations will be able to offer confidential help and advice:

- **The Albany Trust** (Tel: 020-8767 1827)
  They offer one-to-one counselling for people who have been sexually abused or suffer from psychological difficulties.

- **ChildLine** (Tel: 0800-1111)
  A confidential telephone advice for children who are being abused or are at risk.

- **Child Protection in Sport Service (CHILDREN 1ST and sportscotland)**
  (Tel: 0141-418 5674,
  email: cpinsport@children1st.org.uk or
  visit: www.childprotectioninsport.org.uk)
  The Child Protection in Sport Service operates in Scotland and works in partnership with the CPSU to promote consistency and the sharing of good practice across the UK.

- **Child Protection in Sport Unit** (CPSU)
  (Tel: 0116-234 7278 or email: cpsu@nspcc.org.uk)
  This serves as a point of contact for sports clubs/organisations and individuals who need help and advice with safeguarding and child protection issues in sport. Guidance and downloadable materials are available on the website (www.thecpsu.org.uk).

- **Contact Youth** (Tel: 0808-808 8000)
  Youth counselling.

- **Local Rape Crisis Centres**
  These centres offer help to survivors of abuse. You will find the number of your local centre in the telephone directory.

- **Nexus Institute NI** (Tel: 028-9032 6803,
  email: info@nexusinstitute.org or visit
  www.nexusinstitute.org)
  Offers counselling for adult survivors of sexual abuse.

- **NSPCC Child Protection Helpline**
  (Tel: 0808-800 5000)
  A telephone helpline providing advice and support for children who have been abused, and for adults or other children who are concerned that a child has been abused. An online helpline for children is also available (www.achancetotalk.com).

- **Parentline Plus Scotland** (Tel: 0808-800 2222)
  This is a free and confidential helpline for parents and carers. Visit the website at www.parentlineplus.org.uk

National Sports Councils

In addition to seeking the advice of the governing body in your sport, the following organisations will also be able to offer help and advice:

Sport England
3rd Floor, Victoria House
Bloomsbury WC1B 4SE
Tel: 0207-273 1551
Fax: 0207-383 5740
Email: info@sportengland.org
Website: www.sportengland.org

sportscotland
Doges
Templeton on the Green
62 Templeton Street
Glasgow G40 1DA
Tel: 0141-534 6500
Fax: 0141-534 6501
Email: sportscotland.enquiries
@sportscotland.org.uk
Website: www.sportscotland.org.uk

Sports Council for Northern Ireland
House of Sport
2a Upper Malone Road
Belfast BT9 5LA
Tel: 0289-038 1222
Fax: 0289-068 2757
Email: info@sportni.net
Website: www.sportni.net

Sports Council for Wales
Sophia Gardens
Cardiff CF11 9SW
Tel: 0845-045 0904
Fax: 0845-846 0014
Email: scw@scw.co.uk
Website: www.sports-council-wales.co.uk

UK Sport
40 Bernard Street
London WC1N 1ST
Tel: 0207-211 5100
Fax: 0207-211 5246
Email: info@uksport.gov.uk
Website: www.uksport.gov.uk

Other Organisations

Central Registered Body in Scotland
Jubilee House
Forthside Way
Stirling FK8 1QZ
Tel: 01786-849 777
Email: info@crbs.org.uk
Website: www.crbs.org.uk

Child Protection in Sport Service
CHILDREN 1ST
61 Sussex Street
Glasgow G41 1DY
Tel: 0141-418 5674
Fax: 0141-418 5671
Email: cpinsport@children1st.org.uk
Website: www.childprotectioninsport.org.uk

Child Protection in Sport Unit NSPCC National Training Centre
3 Gilmour Close
Beaumont Leys
Leicester LE4 1EZ
Tel: 0116-234 7278
Email: cpsu@nspcc.org.uk
Website: www.thecpsu.org.uk

CHILDREN 1ST
83 Whitehouse Loan
Edinburgh EH9 1AT
Tel: 0131-446 2300
Email: info@children1st.org.uk
Website: www.children1st.org.uk

Criminal Records Bureau
CRB Customer Services
PO Box 165
Liverpool L69 3JD
Tel: 0870-9090 811
Website: www.crb.gov.uk

Department of Health, Social Services and Public Safety Northern Ireland
Castle Buildings
Stormont
Belfast BT4 3SJ
Tel: 0289-052 0500
Email: webmaster@dhsspsni.gov.uk
Website: www.dhsspsni.gov.uk

Disclosure Scotland
PO Box 250
Glasgow G51 1YU
Tel: 0870-609 6006
Fax: 0870-609 6996
Email: info@disclosurescotland.co.uk
Website: www.disclosurescotland.co.uk

NSPCC
Weston House
42 Curtain Road
London EC2A 3NH
Tel: 0207-825 2500
Fax: 0207-825 2525
Email: info@nspcc.org.uk
Website: www.nspcc.org.uk

SkillsActive
Castlewood House
77–91 New Oxford Street
London WC1A 1PX
Tel: 0207-632 2000
Fax: 0207-632 2001
Email: skills@skillsactive.com
Website: www.skillsactive.com

© Andrew Orchard

Feedback – Activity 1

Scenario 1

Ali may have been upset by the fact that the coach didn't seem to be expecting him and that he failed to welcome him to the course. Playing a game of rounders is not a suitable alternative. Ali has booked his place on the tennis course – the coach's solution in this case means that the agreed service has not been provided. As a coach, it is important to consider issues such as resources, facilities and special needs before a session begins.

Scenario 2

In this case, Sandra's mother's personal beliefs will not allow her daughter to take part in a mixed class. Deciding that an excellent alternative would be to allow Sandra to swim with a girls-only class, she has booked this class in advance. It is not until she arrives at the swimming pool that Sandra discovers she cannot attend the class on offer. The coach should have advised Sandra's mother of changes prior to the class being held.

Scenario 3

This is a difficult situation, but no child should be penalised because of his religious beliefs. If the coach maintains this attitude, the children concerned may decide to drop out of the team and the coach may be considered a bully. Under the terms of the Children Act 1989 and the Children (Scotland) Act 1995, all children have the right to be consulted about what they want to do.

Scenario 4

If a coach attempts to lay blame in this way, he is acting in an unprofessional manner. If Jimmy is overweight, the coach should direct him to expert help rather than to make him feel like a victim in front of his fellow team members. This may result in Jimmy giving up the sport with memories of a negative experience.

Scenario 5

Although it is natural for children to get upset if they are given negative feedback, you should never give feedback that is intended to cause upset or humiliation in front of others. Instead, it is important to learn how to provide constructive feedback, and to ensure this is not overheard by other competitors or spectators. This approach will allow children to both acknowledge their strengths and consider how they could improve their performance in future matches.

Remember!

Sport should always be a positive experience for all children. You should:

- treat all individuals in sport with respect at all times

- not discriminate on the grounds of gender, marital status, race, colour, disability, sexuality, age, occupation, religion or political opinion

- not condone, or allow any form of discrimination to go unchallenged

- not publicly criticise or engage in demeaning descriptions of others

- be discreet in any conversations about performers, coaches or other individuals

- communicate with, and provide feedback to, performers in a manner that reflects respect and care.

Feedback – Activity 2

Physical Contact

It is good practice for coaches to inform children, parents and carers that, in some sports, it will be essential for the coach to manually support the child in order for them to perform a technique safely. If this applies to you, you should outline the nature of the support and any further actions that may be necessary if the child needs additional help to perform the technique safely.

Training Practices

In some sports, you may need to explain training practices in detail so that everyone involved in the coaching process understands exactly why and when factors relating to intensity, duration, nutrition or treatment are important.

Language

Always consider the age and experience of the children you are working with. In some cases, it may be appropriate to use technical terminology (when children need to learn the specifics of movements, tactics and rules); in other cases, you may need to simplify the terminology used. Remember that the meaning attached to certain words may vary from region to region. You should try to ensure that the language you use does not confuse children; it should not be a barrier to their understanding and enjoyment of sport.

Player Welfare

The relationship between the child as a young performer, and the child as someone who is able to make decisions relating to their own training, is straightforward in some cases and more delicate in others. You should encourage children to take responsibility for their own development and actions.

Coaching Services

You should discuss and agree on experts or organisations that can offer appropriate further services, with the child and/or parents or carers. Always inform the child and/or parent or carer of any potential costs involved.

Feedback – Activity 3

You may have listed some or all of the following issues:

- Health
- Safety
- Insurance
- Risk assessment
- Paperwork
- Incident forms
- Information for parents
- Consent checks
- Phone numbers
- Professional qualifications
- Being a role model
- Standards of dress and behaviour
- Coach burnout
- Secure storage of information about children
- Photography
- References
- Links with others
- Driving insurance
- First aid.

Feedback – Activity 4

Good practice involves seeking support when you need it. As a coach, you should never feel that you are alone – you should feel able to seek help, advice or support whenever it may help you deal with an issue.

Your diagram may have included some, or all of, the following groups of people. You may like to use the spaces provided to note the names and telephone numbers of specific people in your club/organisation or local area to whom you may turn for help and support.

People Who May Help	Name(s)	Telephone	Email
Club or organisation welfare/child protection officer			
Other coaches in your club/organisation			
Other coaches in your local area			
Friends			
Your line manager			
Head coach			
Development officer/sports development officer			
County development officer			
Regional organiser			
Governing body of sport			
Local leisure authority			
Club committee			
Club employees/caretaker/groundsman			
Parents			
Doctor/dentist			
Social services			
Emergency services (eg fire, police, ambulance)			
Insurance company			
Local newspaper			

Feedback – Activity 6

The committee at Parkgate Sports Club has made every effort to provide a high-quality programme of activities for children that meets standards of good practice.

The many examples of good practice demonstrated in the scenario should contribute to the provision of a positive sporting environment for children – these include:

- providing good club facilities (eg drinking water, telephone, security lighting, overnight security guard)

- not only having a club committee, but having one that is committed to supporting staff, meeting customer needs and providing a safe, secure environment

- reviewing previous activities to identify examples of good practice and areas for improvement

- providing training for committee members and staff

- achieving Clubmark accreditation

- having a designated coaching officer responsible for planning the club's programme of activities

- providing activities for different age groups

- allocating roles and responsibilities to specific staff

- having formal recruitment and induction procedures (including appropriate checks)

- keeping records of children attending the club

- providing orientation sessions for children and their parents/carers

- making every effort to be equitable and to cater for all children, even those with specific needs

- carrying out risk assessments of activities, resources and equipment

- controlling the arrival and departure of people at the club and keeping a register of attendance

- obtaining and acting on customer feedback.

Feedback – Activity 7

This is a very common situation. Young or inexperienced players may often feel that the only way to win is to copy poor behaviour that they have seen elsewhere. In this example, the players on the coach's team felt that they were not going to win without resorting to desperate measures – even though they could be considered to be cheating. They feel that if they 'cheat', they will score goals. They do not associate the concept of 'fair play' with their present situation, but are only focused on the idea of winning.

Feedback – Activity 9

All the scenarios in this activity are examples of situations in which things are not quite right and where a common-sense approach is required. As a coach, it is important to demonstrate exemplary behaviour at all times in order to safeguard athletes and reduce the likelihood of an allegation being made. This involves:

- putting the welfare of your performers first

- treating everyone fairly

- working in an open environment

- maintaining a safe distance from performers and refraining from intimacy (this includes avoiding sharing a room)

- avoiding spending time alone with children away from others – never offer a child a lift home, if this would mean being alone with the child

- building coaching relationships based on trust

- promoting fair play

- being an excellent role model

- involving parents or carers

- giving enthusiastic feedback and avoiding negative criticism.

NB This list is not exhaustive and is by no means definitive.

Poor practice can be harmful for participants, coaches and the club or organisation. It provides a negative model of behaviour and attitude for others, and may lead to misconceptions about the motivation and intent of those involved. It may contribute to creating an environment in which other inappropriate behaviour is accepted or can flourish. Most seriously, poor practice may be part of the grooming process (see page 37) employed by an individual who is motivated to abuse a child.

Sound recruitment processes, the application of codes of practice and prompt reporting of, and responses to, concerns can all contribute to eradicating poor practice and reducing these associated risks.

Feedback – Activity 10

A whole range of emotions may be experienced when faced with possible child abuse. There can sometimes be a self-protective impulse to deny the reality and implications of child abuse. Many people feel emotions such as anger, shock and dismay, perhaps followed by feelings of sadness, sympathy or powerlessness. These feelings are very natural, and it is important to recognise and acknowledge how they may impact on your ability to respond appropriately.

Feedback – Activity 11

You may have found that some of the examples were quite easy to respond to (eg a parent having sexual intercourse with their child is clearly illegal, unacceptable and constitutes abusive behaviour). Some are also covered by legislation – for example, the age of consent for sexual intercourse is 16 years in England, Wales, Ireland and Scotland.

You will probably have found others more difficult and found yourself saying, 'It would depend on...' or, 'I would need to know more about...'. Some of these would not constitute child abuse (eg because of the age of the performer) nor would they contravene legislation. However, they may contravene an ethical code of practice for coaches and others involved in children's sport (eg a coach having a sexual relationship with a 16-year-old performer may constitute an abuse of trust and thus warrant disciplinary action).

Feedback – Activity 12

1 False

Most children who are affected by abuse are abused by adults they know and trust.

2 False

Women also sexually abuse children, although far less than men. In figures for 1998, approximately 5–10% of the perpetrators of sexual abuse of children were women.[25]

3 False

Disabled children are more vulnerable to abuse. They are more dependent on intimate care and sometimes less able to tell anyone or remove themselves from abusive situations. Some adults may also be less likely to hear or believe a disclosure of abuse by a disabled child.

4 False

In 2000, NSPCC figures showed that, in general, the ratios were roughly equal. However, as the following table shows, in the case of serious sexual abuse, overall, girls are more likely to be abused than boys:[26]

Table 1: Incidence of child abuse among under-18s in 2000

Type of Abuse	% of All Boys Under 18 Who Suffered this Type of Abuse in 2000	% of All Girls Under 18 Who Suffered this Type of Abuse in 2000
Serious absence of supervision	6	4
Sexual abuse by parents	1	1
Sexual abuse overall	7	16
Serious physical abuse	6	8

---

[25] Figures taken from the NSPCC report, 'Child Maltreatment in the United Kingdom: A Study of the Prevalence of Child Abuse and Neglect' (2000).

[26] Figures taken from the NSPCC report, 'Child Maltreatment in the United Kingdom: A Study of the Prevalence of Child Abuse and Neglect' (2000).

5 False

Child abuse is unacceptable in all cultures, and there is no government or society that sanctions it. However, there are sometimes differences in how child abuse is defined, and in what may be considered acceptable standards of behaviour towards, and care of, children. Assumptions (particularly those based on stereotypes) about what may be considered acceptable by different groups should not affect a decision to note and report concerns about children's welfare. All residents of the UK must comply with UK legislation regarding children's safeguarding and protection.

6 False

Social services will only remove children when there is a risk of significant harm and if the child is in real danger of further abuse. Social services are there to work in partnership with parents or carers, and to offer as much support as possible. In the minority of cases where it is deemed too unsafe for a child to remain with their parents, consideration is given to placing the child within the wider family network, with fostering or residential care used as a last resort. In 1995, the Department of Health estimated that around 160,000 children were referred to social services departments by all sources because of child protection concerns, and that 96% of those remained in the family home.

7 False

All abuse is harmful. If untreated, the effects of abuse on children can be devastating and may continue into adulthood. The resilience of individual children to abuse is based on a complex combination of personal factors and circumstances (including the support received following disclosure). Assumptions about the impact of abuse on a child, particularly those based on a judgment about the nature or apparent seriousness of their experiences, should be avoided.

8 True

In March 2004, social services' child protection registers for England showed that:

- 40% of children at risk of abuse were less than five years old

- 29% of children at risk of abuse were five to nine years old

- 29% of children at risk of abuse were 10–15 years old

- 2% of children at risk of abuse were aged 16 and over.[27]

9 False

More incidents of child abuse are now reported than 20 years ago because of greater public awareness. However, more adults are now telling others about abuse that occurred during their childhood.

10 False

Children rarely lie about abuse. The common perception that many children invent allegations of abuse is not supported by the experiences of childcare professionals. Many children who experience abuse do not tell anyone. Some children wrongly feel responsible for their abuse, and may want to protect the abuser by denying their experiences. Very often, children have been threatened that something bad will happen if they tell anyone, which means it takes considerable courage for them to disclose their abuse. This makes it vital that children are listened to and taken seriously.

11 True

As organisations have in recent years developed and implemented more effective procedures for staff and volunteers to recognise and report concerns, increasing numbers of cases of sexual, physical or emotional abuse, and bullying and neglect in sport have been reported.

12 True

Some sports situations lend themselves to potential opportunities for emotional abuse, as well as other forms of abuse, to children (eg from the parents whose overwhelming ambition for their child exceeds the aspirations and potential of the child; the coach whose excessive criticism destroys the feelings of confidence and self-worth of the child).

[27] Figures taken from the Department of Education and Skills Statistics for Education: Referrals, Assessments and Children and Young People on Child Protection Registers: Year Ending 31 March 2000 (National Statistics, 2004) (see www.dcsf.gov.uk/rsgateway/index.shtml for further details).

Feedback – Activity 14

In most (if not all) sports, it is possible to identify a range of different issues or practices with the potential to generate child-welfare concerns and may place children at risk of physical harm. Often, the relevant governing body of sport has acknowledged and addressed these issues, usually by issuing specific good-practice guidance for coaches and participants. It may be helpful for you to contact your relevant governing body of sport to raise any issues or concerns that you have identified, and to access any existing guidance that will assist in dealing with these situations. The Child Protection in Sport Unit and CHILDREN 1ST also offer advice and guidance on a range of specific issues through their respective websites www.thecpsu.org.uk and www.childprotectioninsport.org.uk

Feedback – Activity 16

The diagram below shows examples of people who could be responsible for subjecting a child to emotional abuse in your sport. It also indicates some of the questions you should ask yourself to try and identify any situations in which there may be cause for concern.

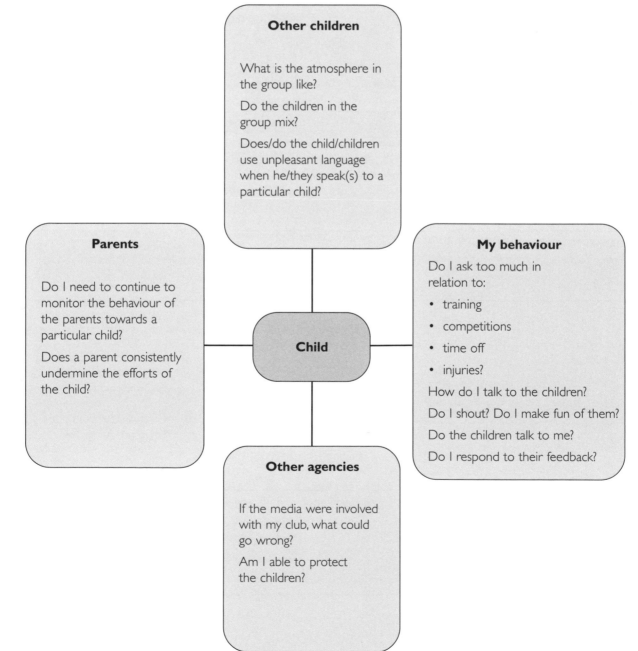

Other children

What is the atmosphere in the group like?

Do the children in the group mix?

Does/do the child/children use unpleasant language when he/they speak(s) to a particular child?

Parents

Do I need to continue to monitor the behaviour of the parents towards a particular child?

Does a parent consistently undermine the efforts of the child?

Child

My behaviour

Do I ask too much in relation to:

• training
• competitions
• time off
• injuries?

How do I talk to the children?

Do I shout? Do I make fun of them?

Do the children talk to me?

Do I respond to their feedback?

Other agencies

If the media were involved with my club, what could go wrong?

Am I able to protect the children?

Feedback – Activity 17

Scenario 1

Some children have a strong desire to maintain privacy. In this case, the child has a skin condition that other children will ask about if they see it and will probably make fun of. By avoiding getting changed in public, this child ensures that the condition remains a secret and maintains the appearance that she is the same as everyone else.

Scenario 2

This scenario is very common. There are several issues here: children often have problems with children from areas other than their own; they like to stick with the friendship groups they have formed already; they will not readily accept changes to teams. Placing the newcomer in a position of authority as a referee causes several further problems. He not only has to demonstrate his rule knowledge and be efficient, but also has to show which team he would prefer to be associated with. Being new is difficult enough without being made to stand out as well. This situation could get worse before it gets better and will require careful handling and monitoring by the coach.

Scenario 3

This scenario exposes players to the unknown. Straight away, several children will feel inadequate and reluctant to play with older players because they don't want to look silly. Others, however, simply may not want to play a mixed game – mixing teams is never easy.

Feedback – Activity 18

1 The main forms of child abuse are explained in the following table:

Category	Explanation
Physical abuse	This includes hitting, burning and biting children; giving children alcohol, inappropriate drugs or poison; attempting suffocate or drown them; providing excessive or inappropriate training regimes; using drugs to enhance performance or delay puberty.
Neglect	Failure to meet a child's basic needs (eg providing them with food, warm clothing); leaving children alone or unsupervised; failure to give love or affection.
Emotional abuse	Persistent lack of love and affection; children being constantly threatened or taunted; parents or coaches whose overwhelming ambition exceeds that of the child; persistent disregard of a child's effort or progress.
Sexual abuse	Where adults or other young people use children to meet their own sexual needs. This includes sexual intercourse, masturbation, oral sex, anal intercourse or fondling, as well as showing children pornographic videos or magazines or taking photos of children for inappropriate use.
Bullying	It is now recognised that, in some cases of abuse, the abuser may not always be an adult, but could be a child. Bullying may be seen as deliberate, hurtful behaviour, usually repeated over a period of time, where it is difficult for those being bullied to defend themselves.

2   **The main effects of abuse on children are as follows:**

- The death of a child.

- Pain and distress.

- Behavioural difficulties, such as becoming angry and aggressive.

- School-related problems.

- Developmental delay – physical, emotional and mental.

- Low self-esteem.

- Depression, self-harm – sometimes leading to suicide.

- Difficulty in forming relationships as adults.

- Sometimes, if untreated, abusive relationships with own (or other) children.

- Temporary or even permanent injury.

3   **Factors that may increase the likelihood of risk:**

- Age – young children may have difficulty telling others.

- Disability – disabled children may have difficulty communicating or accessing people to tell.

- Spending time away from home and family – elite young athletes who are required to spend time away.

- Children already experiencing some form of discrimination (eg racial harassment) – this is a further form of abuse.

- Poor relationship between children and parents/carers.

- High levels of stress.

- History of violence in the family.

If you have had any difficulty with this activity, you may wish to re-read Sections 2.3, 2.4 and 2.5 before moving onto Section 2.6

Feedback – Activity 19

The list you have compiled may cover some or all of the following indicators:

- Unexplained bruising or injuries.

- Sexually explicit actions or language.

- Changes in behaviour or mood.

- Something a child has said.

- A change observed over a long period of time (eg weight loss, increasingly dirty or unkempt).

All these factors are important and children may often suffer from more than one form of abuse. For example, a child who is repeatedly smacked for minor misdemeanours may also experience emotional abuse because they feel frightened, anxious or worthless.

> **Remember!**
>
> Evidence of a combination or repetition of signs over time should alert you to possible problems, not just one bruise.

Feedback – Activity 20

This is a very difficult situation. It is certainly unacceptable for any young person to be left alone overnight, even if quite mature. John may have additional needs – for example, if there was a fire in the house, he would be at increased risk because he may not be able to move as quickly as a non-disabled person. It is an additional concern that John does not know where his dad is, or when he will be back.

The fact that John is left on his own regularly is of concern. A lack of heating is particularly worrying, as John is in a wheelchair and has limited mobility.

The lack of food is difficult to judge. Does this happen all the time or is it unusual? His dad may be due to buy food. If it is a regular occurrence, however, John's basic needs are clearly not being met.

The coach may be concerned that by appearing to interfere in John's family situation, he may damage his relationship with John's dad, and potentially threaten

John's participation in the sport. However, it is important that John's welfare and safety remain the coach's primary concern, and that action is taken to address the identified concerns. It is important that the coach/club/organisation's commitment and approach to safeguarding young participants is communicated to all parties at the outset of a child's involvement, as this can help in dealing with any concerns that arise later. Despite their initial (sometimes angry) reaction to action being taken, many parents come to appreciate that this was ultimately motivated by a genuine desire to protect their children's welfare.

What happened?

Even though John did not mind being alone, the situation he was in was not acceptable. The coach discussed his concerns with the club welfare officer, who consulted social services. John and his dad were contacted, and a social worker visited them at home to discuss the situation and ways the family could be supported. John's dad said they did not want anyone to interfere further. He had not really appreciated John's needs, and thought he had been sufficiently responsible. He agreed not to leave John alone again for such long periods.

Feedback – Activity 21

Minor cuts, bruises and soft tissue injuries (eg strains and tears) are quite common in some sports. The areas where bruising is most likely to occur are the bony parts of the body (eg elbows, knees, shins or forehead).

Remember!

You should be aware of children's injuries or bruising that can only be caused non-accidentally. These will often be part of a recurring pattern, sometimes appearing regularly (eg after a weekend). An important indicator of physical abuse is where bruises or injuries are:

- unexplained or for which multiple or contradictory explanations have been given
- untreated
- inadequately treated (or where there are delays to treatment)
- on parts of the body where accidental injuries are unlikely (eg on the cheeks or thighs).

Bruising may be more or less noticeable on children with different skin tones or from different racial groups. You need to be alert to the following **physical indicators**:

- Unexplained bruising, marks or injuries on any part of the body.
- Bruises that may reflect hand marks or fingertips (from slapping, grabbing, pinching).
- Cigarette burns.
- Bite marks.
- Broken bones (particularly if the child is under two years old).
- Scalds.

Physical abuse may not always be apparent from bruises, fractures or physical signs. **Behavioural indicators**, particularly when there are changes in behaviour, can also indicate that the child is being abused. This might be evident in the following behaviours:

- Fear of parents being contacted.
- Aggressive behaviour or severe temper outbursts.
- Running away.
- Fear of going home (eg after training sessions).
- Flinching when approached or touched.
- Reluctance to get changed for sport.
- Covering arms and legs, even when hot (eg during hard physical activity or in hot weather).
- Depression.
- Withdrawn behaviour.

Feedback – Activity 22

There are a number of reasons why Catherine should be concerned:

- The back of the thigh is an unusual place for marks to appear. It would be improbable that these marks would be caused accidentally. Straight red marks could indicate hand-mark bruising, or having been hit with another straight implement.

- Mrs Carter's behaviour towards Mary may suggest that there is a degree of stress in the family. Mary's distress could be for a number of reasons but it could be clearly linked to what is going on at home. What is important is the change in Mary's usual behaviour.

What happened?

In the end, Catherine was able to talk gently to Mary about why she was upset. It seems that Mrs Carter had lost her temper and slapped Mary hard, leaving marks. Catherine reported her concerns to the sports centre's deputy manager, who has designated responsibility for dealing with safeguarding and child protection concerns. In line with the centre's child protection procedures, he contacted the local social services office to report the concerns and seek advice. A social worker discussed the information with colleagues at the police child protection unit, and Mrs Carter was visited by a social worker and police officer. It transpired that Mr and Mrs Carter had decided to separate and had been under extreme stress in this situation. Social services undertook an assessment of the family's situation and Mary's needs. The police did not feel that taking formal action in relation to Mrs Carter's assault on Mary was appropriate in this case. Mrs Carter was initially very angry and upset that the matter had been reported to the authorities, but subsequently agreed to accept support for her and the family. Social services were able to work with all the family members for a short period of time to help alleviate the stress, and to reduce it's impact on Mary's care and welfare. Mary and Peter continued to attend their swimming lessons at the leisure centre.

Feedback – Activity 23

In sports in which advantages are gained by delaying the onset of puberty (eg the potential strength/weight advantages of prepubescent female gymnasts), drugs and diet may be used to retard physical and sexual development. This may result in serious medical disorders such as anorexia or osteoporosis. In other sports where strength or power are key attributes (eg weight lifting), there is potential abuse from the use of performance-enhancing drugs. In sports where participants qualify to compete in weight-based categories (eg boxing), there can be risks of harm to young competitors who are required to sweat off weight in a very short time shortly before competing. There may be serious medical consequences associated with severe dehydration, together with obvious risks in competing in a weakened condition.

In any sport, there is also the potential for physical abuse from overuse injuries. Children should avoid training or competing when suffering from injury, or before injury or illness rehabilitation has been fully completed.

Feedback – Activity 24

1 You may have mentioned the following issues of concern at this stage:

- The sudden outburst of temper, which is a change of behaviour.
- A reluctance to go home, linked to the dislike of one person.
- The particular vulnerabilities of disabled children in relation to abuse.

2 All these factors may indicate that Carole is being abused. At this stage it would be important to:

- ensure that time is given to Carole, preferably from a female coach, as children who have been abused by a man may prefer to talk to a woman and vice versa
- communicate with her sensitively and comment on the fact that she seems reluctant to go home
- ask if there is anything troubling her as she does not normally get upset
- share any concerns with the centre's child protection officer or a senior colleague.

What happened?

After a long conversation about her worries, Carole eventually told the play worker that Tony had made her touch his genital area. The play worker spoke to the centre manager, who informed social services. The police and social services talked to Carole who told them what was happening. Tony denied the allegation but agreed to leave the family home. Social services continue to work with Carole and her mum, to help Carole overcome the traumatic effect of what happened, and to support Carole during the police's ongoing investigation.

Feedback – Activity 25

1 This is a very difficult situation. Although you may or may not think the way Tom is behaving is abusive, it is clearly unethical, reflects extremely poor practice, and breaches the governing body of sport's code of conduct. The feelings you have will probably range from anger at Tom's behaviour to concern for Kea. You may also feel guilty or frustrated because you have not done anything before now, yet confused because you have known Tom a long time and do not want to risk misconduct proceedings.

2 There are clearly concerns about Tom's behaviour. It is totally unacceptable to touch Kea in the way he did. Even what some may consider to be a friendly gesture (eg putting an arm around the shoulder) may be offensive to some children and could be misconstrued. Likewise, offensive racist comments are in themselves abusive, as are comments which belittle children or make them feel worthless. These are behaviours, which initially may seem less serious than overt physical or sexual abuse. However, they are rarely one-off events and this kind of harassment and bullying of children is just as damaging in the long term.

3 Responding to concerns about a colleague's behaviour is very difficult, particularly if you know the person well, and the consequences of reporting allegations may have far-reaching effects. Equally, it is important to remember that failing to report a colleague may also have far-reaching effects for this child and perhaps others. Poor practice cannot go unchallenged and it may be part of a more serious problem of abuse, which places children at serious risk. It would be important to ensure that Kea is safe and that she is told she is not to blame. It would also be necessary to ensure that Kea and her parents know how to make a complaint. In addition, it would be important to challenge the behaviour with Tom. He may not realise the way he is behaving is offensive. If the behaviour continues or your concerns remain, you must refer the matter to your club welfare officer (or a senior colleague if the club does not yet have a welfare officer). It is their responsibility to contact social services and the police if they judge there is a child protection issue, and/or instigate misconduct or disciplinary proceedings (usually through the governing body of sport). If the concerns are about a senior colleague (or there is no senior colleague), you should refer the matter to the governing body of sport is lead child protection officer or to social services directly. You can also ring the NSPCC Child Protection Helpline for advice (Tel: 0808-800 5000).

What happened?

In this situation, Tom's behaviour was reported to the gymnastics club's welfare officer.

It transpired that this was not the first occasion on which concerns had been expressed about Tom's behaviour and the matter was taken seriously and acted upon immediately. Kea's parents were informed. The club welfare officer sought advice from the governing body of sport and Tom was suspended while misconduct proceedings were begun.

The club welfare officer also referred the matter to the police and social services, and sought their advice. The concerns did not meet the threshold for investigation by the statutory agencies, and the matter was left with the sports organisation to manage within its internal procedures. Under the misconduct proceedings, it was felt that, because Tom was not accepting responsibility for this or previous actions, and refused to acknowledge his behaviour, there was a probability that he would continue to behave in a way that was abusive to children. The club and the governing body of sport therefore did not reinstate him as a coach.

Remember!

In terms of good practice in the care of children, you should never:

- allow or engage in inappropriate touching of any form

- favour one child over others

- make sexually suggestive comments about, or to, a child, even in fun

- refer to a child's ethnicity, disability, gender or sexuality in a way whichis derogatory

- allow children to use inappropriate language unchallenged

- engage in rough, physical or sexually provocative games or horseplay

- do things of a personal nature for children that they can do themselves. If children are very young or are disabled, these tasks should only be carried out with the consent (preferably written) of parents or carers. In an emergency situation, parents or carers should be informed. Discretion and sensitivity are important at all times.[28]

employer (or, if you work in a voluntary capacity, the person responsible for your work) or contact your sport's governing body.

If you are self-employed (or work voluntarily) and work with children at a private venue (eg a gym club in the village hall, athletics session at a college track, football session on the church field, tennis lesson on a friend's private court), there may not be anyone to whom you can report your concerns. If you are in this situation, if there is no one else available or if you are the most senior person, **you will have to take responsibility for taking the next step.** You will need to familiarise yourself with the recommended guidelines and draw up your own code of practice.

You may or may not have obtained any specific guidelines. Whether you are part of a public, private or voluntary body, you have a duty of care (see Appendix C) for the children with whom you work. This means that every organisation should have a policy that clearly states that it is the duty of all those employed or involved to take steps to ensure the safety and to prevent the physical, sexual or emotional abuse of children with whom they come into contact.

Feedback – Activity 27

You may have found this activity easy if you work in a club/organisation that has clear guidelines and procedures to follow when abuse is suspected, and a designated person to whom you can report your concerns (usually the head teacher, club welfare officer, coach, most senior person). It is essential that this designated person is trained and knowledgeable about child protection. If you do not have one already, ask your club/organisation for a copy of its child protection procedures and jot down any further information that you think should be readily available.

However, you may have found the activity quite difficult if either your club/organisation does not currently have any clear procedures or, if it does, you are unaware of them. If this is the case, seek guidance from your

Feedback – Activity 28

Both of these scenarios exist in practice. Case Study 1 shows how, for many, sport manages to exist. However, in this kind of set-up, an accident could be just waiting to happen. Fortunately, some clubs organised on an informal basis, like this one, often develop and adopt the more formal structure of the club described in Case Study 2.

Given the choice, the good practice illustrated in Case Study 2 should be the way forward. Parents and carers have the right to make these choices for their children. In turn, coaches have the opportunity to provide choices that make sport safe for children.

[28] Adapted from *Our Duty to Care* (2006) – this is a useful pack for voluntary organisations to protect children and staff. In addition, *Safe from Harm* (1993) offers a code of practice for safeguarding the welfare of children in voluntary organisations in England and Wales.

Feedback – Activity 29

Every club/organisation should ensure that all reasonable steps are taken to prevent unsuitable people, whether paid or unpaid, from working with children.

The manager of this club made a concerted effort to recruit suitable staff. Examples of good practice include:

- seeking approval from the club committee to recruit extra staff, as it is important that the committee is kept aware of all club activities

- ensuring that the advert contains relevant information about the club and the posts available – this will help to attract the right kind of people

- carrying out a formal application process and asking for a reference

- conducting formal interviews to assess the suitability of the candidates

- making all candidates aware of what will be expected of them

- providing successful candidates with a formal induction to the club and regular feedback on their progress.

In addition to the above, the manager could have:

- contacted the local college for background information on the students that applied for the posts

- asked applicants for two written references, instead of just one

- asked applicants to complete a self-declaration form and required a CRB check

- selected applicants with some or all of the following attributes: first-aid training, child protection training, coaching experience and skill updates

- implemented formal monitoring and appraisal procedures for all club staff, particularly the new recruits.

Feedback – Activity 30

The extracts from the club's records all describe incidents that required a person's response, and which, if left, could have become far more serious and placed children in danger of physical, emotional and sexual abuse or neglect.

Fortunately, the club in question had procedures in place to minimise any damaging or harmful effects in the event of a situation arising in which abuse could occur.

Further ongoing actions could include:

- minimising opportunities for an adult to be left alone with a single child

- providing opportunities for coaches to talk to parents and carers about the expected standards of behaviour of young performers

- introducing clear guidelines and procedures for transporting children; for away and overnight trips and for photography

- arranging for coaches to meet children with their parents and carers present

- coaches encouraging parents and carers to attend training sessions and to support competitions

- carrying out random checks on coaching practice

- encouraging parents and carers to take greater responsibility for ensuring the safety of their children

- introducing a system enabling children with concerns to talk to an independent person outside the club – this person should be given clear written guidelines on the action to take if abuse is disclosed or suspected

- ensuring that agreed procedures for protecting children apply to all staff (whether paid or voluntary, full- or part-time, permanent or temporary). This should include:

  - ensuring that all staff have clear roles and responsibilities

  - issuing guidelines on the action to take if abuse is disclosed or suspected

  - implementing a supervision and appraisal system that monitors roles and relationships, and observes coaching practice.

Measures such as these not only protect the children, but also protect coaches by reducing the likelihood of accusations of improper behaviour being made.

What are the Criminal Records Bureau and Disclosure Scotland?

The Criminal Records Bureau (CRB) and Disclosure Scotland were set up by the Home Office and the Scottish Executive respectively to improve access to criminal record checks for organisations making decisions about the employment and deployment of staff and volunteers whose role involves responsibility for, or contact with, children and/or vulnerable adults. In particular, it contributes to the safeguarding and protection of children and vulnerable adults from those who may represent a risk to them.

In Wales, the Wales Council for Voluntary Action Criminal Records Unit (CRU) is funded by the Welsh Assembly Government. The CRU provides an umbrella service, and free access to disclosures for voluntary organisations, including a number of governing bodies of sport.

Some sporting clubs and organisations already include the requirement for criminal records checks for those involved with, or responsible for, children and young people[30] as part of their recruitment and selection process. As recommended in Section 1.3 of this pack, all sport and leisure providers should adopt this practice as part of an overall child protection policy.

Given the number of adults involved in either a paid or voluntary capacity in sporting clubs/organisations, obtaining, processing and storing criminal records disclosure information will be a huge task. The aim of this appendix is to give guidance to sports clubs, organisations and governing bodies of sport on how to approach this task.

It is important to remember that accessing and assessing criminal records disclosure information should form only part of a comprehensive process for recruiting and deploying suitable staff and volunteers, as outlined in Section 1.3.

© Alan Edwards

---

[29] Adapted with kind permission from the Criminal Records Bureau and the Child Protection in Sport Unit.

[30] While the information provided by the CRB is important in terms of recruitment and selection, organisations must recognise that this is only one of a much wider series of steps that need to be taken in order to create and sustain a safe environment for children. These steps are outlined in Sections One, Two and Three of this pack.

When Should Someone be Checked?

The CRB provides a service to employers and volunteering groups in England and Wales[32] of all kinds called 'disclosure'. In Scotland, this service is provided by Disclosure Scotland. The employer will be able to use the Disclosure service to help establish whether a successful candidate has a recorded background that might make them unsuitable for the position in question.

As well as using this service to check the background of new candidates, clubs and organisations should consider whether existing staff or volunteers should also be CRB checked. This is especially important if an individual is being considered for a change in role that increases their contact with children, or is subject to an investigation within disciplinary procedures as a result of concerns about their behaviour towards children or young people.

This procedure will need to be implemented carefully within a club or organisation, and may require amendments to current organisational or governing body of sport constitutions. It is important that the context for this action is fully communicated to all those involved in the sport and that issues of confidentiality are fully detailed. You will need to consider who within the organisation or governing body of sport will communicate this to staff and volunteers, and who will hold the information and make sure that this process complies with data protection legislation.

One option that you may wish to consider is to use a declaration as a means of implementing this procedure, such as the following statement:

*From (date), the organisation/governing body of (sport) adopted a child protection policy. This policy will ensure that (organisation) takes all necessary steps to promote a safe atmosphere for all children and young people involved in (sport). All those currently involved with (sport) with significant contact with children will be required to give an assurance that they have no previous criminal convictions that could put children at risk. This information is **strictly confidential** except for the legal obligation of reporting child abuse.*

The applicant initiates the disclosure check and both the applicant and the employer receive copies of the disclosure. You should notify applicants of your intention to seek a disclosure. A suggested statement to be included on all application forms is:

This post involves substantial access to children. As a club/organisation, we are committed to the welfare and protection of children. All applications to work with us in either a voluntary or paid capacity will involve a criminal records check.

If a club or organisation knowingly appoints a person who is banned from working with children, they will be committing a criminal offence, as will the individual by applying for a role that involves working with children. In England and Wales, under the Protection of Children Act 1999, voluntary clubs and organisations are encouraged to report their concerns, while registered children's clubs and organisations are obliged to report concerns. In Scotland, the Protection of Children (Scotland) Act 2003 obliges all organisations to refer their concerns.

Level of Disclosure

Although when the CRB was established, the government intended to provide three levels of disclosure, the Basic level was never introduced, and only Standard and Enhanced levels are available.

What checks are provided?

Standard- and Enhanced-level Checks note:

- all convictions, cautions, reprimands or formal warnings held on the Police National Computer (PNC)

- information from the Protection of Children Act List (PoCA)

- information from the Protection of Vulnerable Adults List (POVA)

- information held by the DfES under Section 142 of the Education Act 2002 as considered unsuitable for, and banned from, working with children.

[32] For information about Disclosure services in Scotland, telephone 0141-585 8400 or visit www.disclosurescotland.co.uk, and in Northern Ireland, telephone 028-9052 0500 or visit www.dhsspsni.gov.uk

100

Enhanced-level Checks also include:

- local police force information (including 'soft' – non-conviction – information) considered relevant by chief police officer(s).

It is up to each applying body to determine the appropriate level of disclosure. In Scotland, those who hold a 'childcare position' are required to undertake an enhanced criminal records check. This includes coaches and volunteers who come into contact with children through sport. Following the Bichard enquiry into the employment of Ian Huntley, the CRB has advised organisations to access Enhanced-level Disclosures for staff and volunteers with roles that involve contact with or responsibility for children and young people.

Please note: applications for the Standard and Enhanced Disclosures can only be made through a body that is registered with the CRB. The registered body must adhere to the CRB Code of Practice and ensure confidentiality. When a disclosure is issued, a copy is sent to both the registered body and the individual concerned.

More detailed information is available for England and Wales from the CRB and the Child Protection in Sport Unit (CPSU), and for Scotland from Disclosure Scotland and the Central Registered Body in Scotland:

Central Registered Body in Scotland
Jubilee House
Forthside Way
Stirling FK8 1QZ
Tel: 01786-849 777
Email: info@crbs.org.uk
Website: www.crbs.org.uk

Child Protection in Sport Unit
NSPCC National Training Centre
3 Gilmour Close
Beaumont Leys
Leicester LE4 1EZ
Tel: 0116-234 7278
Email: cpsu@nspcc.org.uk
Website: www.thecpsu.org.uk

Criminal Records Bureau
CRB Customer Services
PO Box 165
Liverpool L69 3JD
Tel: 0870-90 90 811
Website: www.crb.gov.uk

Disclosure Scotland
PO Box 250
Glasgow G51 1YU
Tel: 0870-609 6006
Fax: 0870-609 6996
Email: info@disclosurescotland.co.uk
Website: www.disclosurescotland.co.uk

© Alan Edwards

APPENDIX B:
National Occupational Standards for Coaching, Teaching and Instructing

The National Occupational Standards for Coaching, Teaching and Instructing (NOS for CTI) are based around a number of competences associated with planning, delivering and evaluating coaching sessions and programmes. The standards are used as part of sports governing bodies' coach education awards and as the definition of competence for National/Scottish Vocational Qualifications (N/SVQs) in coaching, teaching and instructing. N/SVQs at Levels 2 and 3 are available in a number of sports. sports coach UK has developed its Coach Development Programme around these standards. Their workshops and packs aim to provide the underpinning knowledge for coaches who wish to meet the competences of the standards. They also give coaches guidelines on how to apply this knowledge to their coaching practice.

Safeguarding and Protecting Children: A guide for sportspeople has been designed to support the following unit of the Level 2/3 NOS:

Unit C36	**Support the protection of children from abuse**
C36.1	Report signs of possible abuse
C36.2	Respond to a child's disclosure of abuse

For further information about the National Occupational Standards for Coaching, Teaching and Instructing at Level 2/3, contact sports coach UK or SkillsActive at the following addresses:

sports coach UK
114 Cardigan Road
Headingley
Leeds LS6 3BJ
Tel: 0113-274 4802
Fax: 0113-275 5019
Email: coaching@sportscoachuk.org
Website: www.sportscoachuk.org

SkillsActive
Castlewood House
77–91 New Oxford Street
London WC1A 1PX
Tel: 0207-632 2000
Fax: 0207-632 2001
Email: skills@skillsactive.com
Website: www.skillsactive.com

© South Yorkshire Sport

© Alex Handley

APPENDIX C:
Further Information on the National Strategies, Legislation and Guidance

Contents

England

- Every Child Matters: Change for Children (ECM)
- 'Working Together to Safeguard Children' (revised 2006)
- Local Safeguarding Children Boards
- Vetting and Barring Scheme
- Information Sharing
- Common Core of Skills and Knowledge
- Common Assessment Framework

Northern Ireland

- Children (NI) Order 1995
- Our Children and Young People – Our Pledge (2006)
- Co-operating to Safeguard Children (2003)
- Sexual Offences Order (Consultation ended October 2006)
- Criminal Law Act (NI) 1967
- Police Act 1997
- Protection of Children and Vulnerable Adults (NI) Order 2003 (POCVA)
- Understanding the Needs of Children in Northern Ireland (UNOCINI)
- ACCESS NI
- Further Reading

Scotland

- Vision for Children
- Children's Hearing System
- Child Protection Reform Programme
- Vetting and Barring Scheme
- Local Child Protection Committees (CPCs)
- Getting it Right for Every Child

Wales

- Children and Young People: Rights to Action
- Climbing Higher and Safeguarding Vulnerable Children Review
- Safeguarding Children: Working Together under the Children Act 2004
- Local Safeguarding Children Boards
- Vetting and Barring Scheme
- Information Sharing
- All Wales Child Protection Procedures

CPSU Guidance: Duty of Care

England

Every Child Matters: Change for Children (ECM)

Aims and Outcomes

Every Child Matters: Change for Children is a new approach to ensuring the well-being of all children and young people. The government's aim is for every child, whatever their background or their circumstances, to have the support they need to:

- be healthy
- stay safe
- enjoy and achieve
- make a positive contribution
- achieve economic well-being.

This means that the organisations involved with providing services to children – from hospitals and schools, to police and voluntary groups – will be collaborating in new ways, sharing information and working together, to protect children and young people from harm and to help them achieve what they want from life. Children and young people will have far more say about issues that affect them as individuals and collectively.

Over the next few years, every local authority will be working with its partners, through children's trusts, to find out what works best for children and young people in its area and then act on it. They will need to involve children and young people in this process and, when inspectors assess how local areas are doing, they will pay particular attention to the views of children and young people themselves.

Culture, Sport, Play

When asked what they regard as their priorities, children and young people consistently reply that they would like more 'things to do and places to go'. The Department for Culture, Media and Sport (DCMS) is working to improve access to culture, sport and play for children and young people, so that they can develop their talents and enjoy the benefits of participation.

Culture, sport and play organisations have a unique role to play in helping to deliver the Every Child Matters: Change for Children agenda, by:

- delivering the five outcomes – particularly 'enjoy and achieve' and 'make a positive contribution'

- being key partners in children's trusts and contributing to Children and Young People's Plans

- supporting families and promoting diversity

- reaching millions of children and young people through positive out-of-school activities.

The DCMS works through its sponsored bodies to mobilise the national culture, sport and play networks to deliver change for children.

The Government Youth Green Paper, 'Youth Matters, the Every Child Matters strategy for young people' was published in July 2005. 'Youth Matters: Next Steps', published in March 2006, sets out the vision for empowering young people, giving them somewhere to go, something to do and someone to talk to. The aim is for young people to have more choice and influence over services and facilities that are available to them. The government also wants to encourage young people to volunteer and contribute to their local community. There is a major focus on the sports sector within the 'Youth Matters: Next Steps' document.

Further information on the government's Every Child Matters strategy and on Youth Matters can be found at www.everychildmatters.gov.uk

'Working Together to Safeguard Children' (revised 2006) HM Government

'Working Together to Safeguard Children' is a key guidance document for all organisations providing services for, or working with, children and young people. It sets out how organisations and individuals should work together to safeguard and promote the welfare of children. Part I of the document comprises statutory guidance, while Part II is non-statutory practice guidance.

1.18 **Safeguarding and promoting the welfare of children** is defined for the purposes of this guidance as:

- protecting children from maltreatment (abuse and neglect)

- preventing impairment of children's health or development

- ensuring that children are growing in circumstances consistent with the provision of effective care

- undertaking that role so as to enable those children to have optimum life chances and to enter adulthood successfully.

1.20 **Child protection** is part of safeguarding and promoting welfare. This refers to the activity that is undertaken to protect specific children who are suffering, or at risk of suffering, significant harm.

Key sections for sports organisations, staff and volunteers:

1.16 For those children who are suffering, or at risk of suffering, significant harm, joint working is essential to safeguard and promote the welfare of the child(ren) and, where necessary, to bring to justice the perpetrators of crimes against children.

All agencies and professionals should:
- be alert to potential indicators of abuse or neglect

- be alert to the risks which individuals abusers, or potential abusers, may pose to children

- share and help to analyse information so that an assessment can be made of the child's needs and circumstances

- contribute to whatever actions are needed to safeguard and promote the child's welfare

- take part in regularly reviewing the outcomes for the child against specific plans

- work cooperatively with parents unless this is inconsistent with ensuring the child's safety.

2.151 **Organisations in the voluntary and private sectors that work with children need to have the arrangements described in paragraph 2.8 (see below) in place** in the same way as organisations in the public sector, and need to work effectively with LSCBs. Paid and volunteer staff need to be aware of their responsibilities for safeguarding and promoting the welfare of children and how they should respond to child protection concerns in line with guidance (summarised in 'What to do if You're Worried a Child is Being Abused'.)

2.8 To fulfil their commitment to safeguard and promote the welfare of children, **all organisations that provide services for children, or work with children, need to have in place:**

- clear priorities for safeguarding and promoting the welfare of children explicitly stated in strategic policy documents

- a clear commitment by senior management to the importance of safeguarding and promoting children's welfare

- a clear line of accountability within the organisation for work on safeguarding and promoting the welfare of children

- recruitment and human resources management procedures that take account of the need to safeguard and promote the welfare of children and young people, including arrangements for appropriate checks on new staff and volunteers

- procedures for dealing with allegations of abuse against members of staff and volunteers

- arrangements to ensure that all staff undertake appropriate training to equip them to carry out their responsibilities effectively, and keep this up to date through refresher training at regular intervals; and that all staff, including temporary staff and volunteers who work with children, are made aware of the establishment's arrangements for safeguarding and promoting the welfare of children and their responsibilities for that

- have policies in place for safeguarding and promoting the welfare of children (for example, pupils/students), including a child protection policy, and procedures that are in accordance with guidance from the local authority and locally agreed inter-agency procedures

- have arrangements in place to work effectively with other organisations to safeguard and promote the welfare of children, including arrangements for sharing information

- a culture of listening to, and engaging in dialogue with, children – seeking their views in ways appropriate to their age and understanding, and taking account of those both in individual decisions and the establishment or development of services

- appropriate whistle-blowing procedures and a culture that enables issues about safeguarding and promoting the welfare of children to be addressed.

Sport, Culture and Leisure Services

2.23 Sport and cultural services designed for children and families such as libraries, play schemes and play facilities, parks, and gardens, sport and leisure centres, events and attractions, museums and arts centres are directly provided, purchased or grant-aided by local authorities, the commercial sector and by community and voluntary organisations. Many such activities take place in premises managed by authorities or their agents.

2.24 Staff, volunteers and contractors who provide these services will have various degrees of contact with children who use them, and appropriate arrangements will need to be in place. These should include:

- procedures for staff and others to report concerns that they may have about the children they meet that are in line with 'What to do if you are worried a child is being abused' and LSCB (local safeguarding children board) procedures, as well as arrangements such as those described above

- appropriate codes of practice for staff, particularly sports coaches, such as those issued by national governing bodies of sport, the Health and Safety Executive or the local authority. Sports organisations can also seek advice on child protection issues from the Child Protection in Sport Unit (CPSU), which has been established as a partnership between the NSPCC and Sport England.

'Working Together to Safeguard Children' (2006) can be downloaded from: www.everychildmatters.gov.uk/socialcare/safeguarding/workingtogether/

Local Safeguarding Children Boards (LSCBs)

Every local area now needs to have an LSCB in place. Guidance on local safeguarding children boards forms Chapter 3 of 'Working Together to Safeguard Children'. For further information, visit: www.everychildmatters.gov.uk/socialcare/safeguarding/workingtogether/

Vetting and Barring Scheme

The Bichard Inquiry Report made a number of recommendations about changes to the way in which applicants for posts that involve working with children will be vetted. In January 2006, the Secretary of State for Education announced legislation to introduced a new centralised vetting and barring system for people whose jobs will bring them into contact with children and vulnerable adults. The Safeguarding Vulnerable Groups Bill (which relates to both children and vulnerable adults) is passing through parliament and is anticipated to become law before the new scheme is planned to be in operation in 2007/08.

Further information about the planned vetting and barring scheme is available at www.isa.homeoffice.gov.uk

Information Sharing

Sharing information is vital for early intervention to ensure that children and young people get the services they require. It is also essential to protect children and young people from suffering harm from abuse or neglect and to prevent them from offending. There has been confusion and uncertainty on the part of many professionals and volunteers working with children in all sectors, about when, how, and with whom concerns about the welfare or safety of children may be shared with others.

Following consultation, the government has developed and published guidance for immediate use by all practitioners who work with children or young people – employed or volunteering, working in the public, private or voluntary sectors. 'Information Sharing: Practitioners' Guide' (2006) comprises three main parts:

- Core guidance – giving practitioners clear, practical guidance, drawing on experience and the public consultation.

- A set of case examples which illustrate information sharing situations.

- A summary of the laws affecting information sharing in respect of children and young people.

For further information, or to download the guidance, go to www.everychildmatters.gov.uk/deliveringservices/informationsharing/

Common Core of Skills and Knowledge

The Common Core of Skills and Knowledge for the Children's Workforce sets out the basic skills and knowledge needed by people (including volunteers) whose work brings them into regular contact with children, young people and families. It will enable multi-disciplinary teams to work together more effectively in the interests of the child.

The skills and knowledge are described under six main headings:

- Effective communication and engagement with children, young people and families

- Child and young person development

- Safeguarding and promoting the welfare of the child

- Supporting transitions

- Multi-agency working

- Sharing information.

Over time, the government expects everyone working with children, young people and families (including those working in a paid or voluntary capacity within sport) to be able to demonstrate a basic level of competence in the six areas of the Common Core. In the future, the Common Core will form part of qualifications for working with children, young people and families and it will act as a foundation for training and development programmes run by employers and training organisations. When further guidance has been issued on the application of the Common Core for different parts of the children's workforce, all safeguarding and child protection training will be reviewed and, if necessary, revised to ensure that the requirements of the Common Core are met.

Visit www.dfes.gov.uk for further information on, or to download the Common Core of Skills and Knowledge go to www.everychildmatters.gov.uk/delivering services/commoncore

Common Assessment Framework for Children and Young People

The Common Assessment Framework (CAF) is a key part of delivering front-line services that are integrated and focused around the needs of children and young people. The CAF is a standardised approach to conducting an assessment of a child's additional needs and deciding how those needs should be met. It can be used by practitioners across children's services in England.

The CAF will promote more effective, earlier identification of additional needs, particularly in universal services. It is intended to provide a simple process for a holistic assessment of a child's needs and strengths, taking account of the role of parents, carers and environmental factors on their development. Practitioners will then be better placed to agree, with

the child and family, what support is appropriate. The CAF will also help to improve integrated working by promoting coordinated service provision. All local authority areas are expected to implement the CAF between April 2006 and the end of 2008.

Further information on the 'Common Assessment Framework' can be found at www.everychildmatters.gov.uk/deliveringservices/caf/

Northern Ireland

Much of the legislation and guidance in place in Northern Ireland and referenced below mirrors equivalent legislation and guidance in England. Legislation and guidance are constantly changing and this briefing is correct at the time of going to print (March 2007). For any further updates, please contact the Child Protection in Sport Unit in Northern Ireland (Tel: 028-9035 1135).

The Children (NI) Order 1995

The Children (NI) Order 1995 is the **key** piece of legislation; it deals with public and private law about children in Northern Ireland and is the equivalent of the Children Act (1989) in England. It is based on five key principles:

The Children Act (2004) in England and Wales is not currently mirrored in Northern Ireland, but the Department of Health, Social Services and Public Safety (DHSSPS) is to consult on an Adoption and Children

These are the cornerstone principles of good practice	• Paramountcy	The welfare of the child shall be the paramount consideration in any decision made.
	• Parental Responsibility	Parents have responsibilities towards their children rather than rights over them. A wider range of people can now have parental responsibility.
	• Prevention	Preventing children from being abused and supporting them to promote their health and welfare.
	• Partnership	The best way of meeting children's needs is to work with parents and carers, and for agencies to work together.
	• Protection	There is a duty to investigate where a child is at risk of significant harm because of a lack of care or actual abuse.

(NI) Order that will also include legislation to introduce a Local Safeguarding Children Board (LSCB), which is not currently established in Northern Ireland.

The intention is to strengthen inter-agency cooperation on child protection through the establishment of a new Northern Ireland Safeguarding Children Board (replacing the four Area Child Protection Committees). This will ensure cooperation on child protection and safeguarding arrangements at the highest level within government departments, local government and in the statutory, voluntary and community sectors.

It will have an independent chair and clear accountability lines to ministers. The consultation on the establishing of a Northern Ireland LSCB closed in February 2007.

The current role of the Area Child Protection Committees (ACPCs) in Northern Ireland is to develop a strategic approach to child protection within the overall Children's Services Planning process. Included within these responsibilities is the requirement to monitor and evaluate, on a regular and continuing basis, how well services work together to protect children, and to ensure that a specific report on outcomes is conveyed to the board, trusts, constituent agencies of ACPC and professional groups.

Our Children and Young People - Our Pledge (2006)

The aim of this strategy (the equivalent of 'Every Child Matters' in England) is to ensure that, by 2016, all children and young people are fulfilling their potential. The government want those children who are doing well to continue to do well. However, there is evidence that, despite significant investment by government over many years, there is insufficient progress being made to improve the lives of our most marginalised and disadvantaged children and young people.

The following six outcomes form the strategy. Children have the right to be:

- healthy
- enjoying, learning and achieving
- living in safety and with stability
- experiencing economic and environmental well-being
- contributing positively to community and society
- living in a society that respects their rights.

Co-operating To Safeguard Children (2003)

This guidance mirrors 'Working Together to Safeguard Children' in England.

The DHSSPS document provides child protection guidelines and outlines the roles and responsibilities of all agencies. There are particular sections that medical staff should to be aware of.

Sexual Offences Order (Consultation ended October 2006)

When the Sexual Offences Act (2003) was passed by Parliament in 2003, a number of new child sex offences included in it were not extended to Northern Ireland. It is now intended to ensure that children in Northern Ireland will receive the same protection as those in England and Wales. The Minister of State, Northern Ireland Office, has announced that the Sexual Offences Order is timetabled to go through parliament before summer 2007. This will see the creation of new offences and increased tariffs for those who harm children. Part 2 of the act was implemented in Northern Ireland in 2003 and focused on the registration and management of those convicted of sexual offences.

The Criminal Law Act (NI) 1967

This is Northern Ireland-specific legislation with no equivalent elsewhere in the UK. It outlines the community's responsibility in reporting child abuse. It states:

Anyone with direct knowledge or information about an arrestable offence, is required to inform the police within a reasonable time. An arrestable offence may include the non-disclosure of serious cases of child abuse.

Police Act 1997

What is known as Part 5 of the Police Act 1996 was not implemented in Northern Ireland. The Northern Ireland Office plan to enact this piece of the legislation by summer 2007. This will enable the Police Service Northern Ireland to disclose what is termed 'soft intelligence' (ie non-conviction information) when they deem it appropriate. This will coincide with the establishment of Access NI, the equivalent to the Criminal Record Bureau in England and Wales.

The Protection of Children and Vulnerable Adults (NI) Order 2003 (POCVA)

The POCVA mirrors the Protection of Children Act (1999) in England and Wales and has enhanced the arrangements for safeguarding vulnerable members of society.

The new Protection Of Children and Vulnerable Adults (NI) Order (POCVA) became law in February 2003 but became operational (with the exception of Article 46) in April 2005. POCVA aims to improve existing safeguards for children and vulnerable adults by preventing unsuitable people working with them in any capacity, whether paid or unpaid. POCVA complements each agency's own child protection measures and all agencies entrusted with the care of children need to have robust recruitment and staff selection procedures, which are enhanced after appointment by appropriate training, supervision and appraisal processes.

Understanding the Needs of Children in Northern Ireland (UNOCINI)

This legislation is an equivalent of the Framework for the Assessment of Children in Need and their Families in England. The DHSSPS completed a consultation in 2006 on the development of an Assessment Framework and are due to begin multi-agency staff training on this framework in April 2007.

UNOCINI will be used to make referrals to social services. Using UNOCINI will ensure that children being referred come with the wealth of information that has already been collected by professionals working with them. This will mean that children and their families will not need to go through the same questions with the social worker that others have already asked.

ACCESS NI (due to be implemented by the end of 2007)

ACCESS NI is a new system for the disclosure of an individual's criminal history. It is being established by the Northern Ireland Office as a result of the introduction in Northern Ireland of Part V of the Police Act 1997 and will replace the current system of pre-employment checking administered by the DHSSPS.

Employers will be required to register with ACCESS NI to become a 'registered body'. There will be a fee of approximately £150 per organisation to register. This will include the registration of one counter signatory. This person will undergo the equivalent of an Enhanced Check (see below). An additional fee will be levied for each additional counter signatory, who will also undergo an enhanced check.

There will be **three** different levels of disclosure. Individuals will be able to access a Basic Disclosure. Registered employers can only access Standard and Enhanced Disclosures.

1. Basic Disclosure

An individual may apply for their own criminal record certificate, which will disclose any unspent convictions recorded on police systems.

2. Standard Disclosure

An employer seeking to employ a person in the occupations listed in the Exceptions Order to the Rehabilitation of offenders (NI) Order 1978, is eligible for a **Standard** or **Enhanced** Disclosure. All **regulated positions** under the Protection of Children and Vulnerable Adults (NI) Order 2003 will be subject to an **Enhanced Disclosure**.

This level of disclosure will provide criminal record information, including spent and unspent convictions and cautions. If the post involves work with vulnerable groups, it will also provide UK Disqualification List information. It will not provide soft intelligence information.

3. Enhanced Disclosure

This level of disclosure will provide NI and GB criminal records, including spent convictions and UK Disqualification List information:

- Disqualification from Working with Children List (NI)

- Disqualification from Working with Vulnerable Adults List (NI)

- Protection of Children Act List (E/W)

- Protection of Vulnerable Adults List (E/W)

- Disqualification from Working with Children List (Scotland)

- Unsuitable Persons List (UK)

It will also provide UK Soft Intelligence.

All regulated positions under the Protection of Children and Vulnerable Adults (NI) Order 2003 will be subject to an Enhanced Disclosure.

Scotland

Vision for Children

The Scottish Executive has agreed a vision for Scotland's children that provides the overarching context for the development of policy. The vision is that Scotland's children should be:

- safe

- nurtured

- healthy

- active

- respected and responsible

- achieving

- included.

Many of the national guidance documents relating to safeguarding children are of interest and relevance in Scotland. The principles underpinning these documents also apply in Scotland. Every home country should be aware of, and respond to, the findings of any inquiries into the death or significant harm caused to a child – regardless of where they live. However, responsibility for the care, welfare and protection of Scotland's children and young people is devolved to the Scottish Parliament. The Scottish Executive therefore leads on issuing national policy, guidance and legislation that reflect national and local structures and the Scottish legal system, which includes the Children's Hearing System.

Children's Hearing System

For more information on the Children's Hearing System, visit www.chscotland.gov.uk

In 2000, following the report into the death of a child called Kennedy McFarlane, Scottish Ministers ordered an audit and review of child protection across Scotland. The aim of the review was to promote the reduction of abuse and neglect of children and to improve services for children who experience abuse and neglect. While the primary focus of this audit and review was the work of agencies, such as health, police, education and social work, it also took in to consideration the general publics' views of child protection.

Child Protection Reform Programme

The findings of the audit and review were reported in 'It's Everyone's Job to Make Sure I'm Alright' (Scottish Executive, 2002). The title of the report represents the view of one child interviewed as part of the review. The Child Protection Review Team made a number of recommendations to improve the system, including ensuring the public have access to information about how to access help for children for whom they are worried. The Scottish Executive responded to these findings by initiating a three-year Child Protection Reform Programme. Some of the outcomes of this Programme include the following:

1. 'Protecting Children and Young People – Framework for Standards'. This sets out what each child in Scotland can expect from professionals and agencies to ensure that they are adequately protected and their needs are met. It also sets out what parents or other adults who may report abuse and neglect can expect.

2. A Children's Charter setting out what children and young people can expect to help keep them safe from harm.

3. Guidance on the composition, role and responsibilities of Child Protection Committees.

4. A system of multi-disciplinary inspections of agencies providing services for children and young people.

5   An Integrated Assessment Framework designed to adopt a multi-agency approach towards the assessment of children who are in need or who may require care and protection.

6   New legislation, including the Protection of Children (Scotland) Act 2003, intended to improve the safeguards available for the recruitment and selection of staff and volunteers who work with children and young people.

7   A public awareness campaign.

8   Action to improve the range and quality of training available.

The outcomes of the Child Protection Reform Programme apply to all sectors – public, private and voluntary, including sport. They reinforce responsibilities highlighted in 'Protecting Children – A Shared Responsibility' (Scottish Office, 1998) that:

Voluntary organisations and statutory agencies, including the police and health services should work together to develop good relationships. Voluntary organisations should discuss and share with relevant statutory agencies information they may have about children who may be at risk of significant harm. Statutory agencies should, where appropriate, provide advice and support to voluntary organisations in promoting effective child protection practice in their organisation.

Vetting and Barring Scheme

The Bichard Inquiry Report made a number of recommendations for changes to the way in which applicants for posts that involve working with children will be vetted. The Protection of Vulnerable Groups (Scotland) Bill 2006 is expected to become law in 2007 and provides for the establishment of the new Scottish Vetting and Barring Scheme. The Scheme builds on some of the existing provisions of the Protection of Children (Scotland) Act 2003.

Local Child Protection Committees (CPCs)

CPCs are the key inter-agency strategic vehicles for child protection work in each local authority. The voluntary sector, including sport and leisure, should be represented on each CPC. What is expected of a CPC is set out in Scottish Executive guidance (available at www.scotland.gov.uk/childprotection).

Further information on CPC guidance is available at www.scotland.gov.uk/publications/2005/02/20675/52303

Getting it Right for Every Child

Getting it Right for Every Child is the Scottish Executive's reform programme for children's services. It is an approach that puts children and young people at the centre of services and makes them a key part of finding solutions to their needs. The programme aims to ensure that:

-   every child deserves the best possible start in life

-   every child deserves the same opportunities

-   every child should get the help they need when they need it.

The Children's Services (Scotland) Bill 2007 is intended to support the reform of children's services. The outcome of this legislation is likely to be a duty on agencies to promote the well-being of children and to work together. The Bill also proposes measures to ensure the views of children are taken into account and changes to the grounds for referring a child to the Children's Hearings system.

Further information about the Getting It Right for Every Child is available at www.scotland.gov.uk/Topics/People/Young-People/childrensservices/background/girfec

For more information on child protection in Scotland, visit www.scotland.gov.uk/childprotection or contact:

Child Protection in Sport Service
CHILDREN 1ST
61 Sussex Street
Glasgow G41 1DY
Tel: 0141-418 5674
Email: cpinsport@children1st.org.uk

Wales

Children and Young People: Rights to Action

Published by the Welsh Assembly Government in 2004, 'Children and Young People: Rights to Action' (January 2004) is the Welsh equivalent to 'Every Child Matters'. The strategy sets out the future direction of policy relating to children and young people and also how the Welsh Assembly Government intended to implement provision in the Children Act 2004.

Section 25 (2) of the Children Act 2004 sets out five core aims for safeguarding and promoting the welfare of children and young people in Wales. Children should:

- be healthy

- stay safe

- enjoy and achieve

- make a positive contribution

- achieve economic well-being.

In Wales, these five outcomes are also embodied in the Welsh Assembly Government's seven Core Aims, which are based on the United Nations Convention on the Rights of the Child. The aims are to ensure that all children and young people in Wales:

- have a flying start

- have a comprehensive range of education and learning opportunities

- enjoy the best possible health and are free from abuse, victimisation and exploitation

- have access to play, leisure, sporting and cultural activities

- are listened to, treated with respect, and have their race and cultural identity recognised

- have a safe home and community that supports physical and emotional well-being

- are not disadvantaged by poverty.

The fourth aim, relating to all children and young people having access to play, leisure, sporting and cultural activities, has a section within 'Rights to Action' (pp41–48) and is further discussed with the Welsh Assembly Government's sport strategy 'Climbing Higher'.

Climbing Higher and Safeguarding Vulnerable Children Review

'Climbing Higher' was published by the Welsh Assembly Government in July 2003 and sets out the long-term strategy for sport and physical activity in Wales. The strategy makes specific reference to safeguarding by stating:

All of this must happen within an ethical framework of respect and fairness that fully protects and safeguards the rights of children.

('Climbing Higher', Welsh Assembly Government, July 2003, p.14).

The Safeguarding Vulnerable Children Review was established by First Minister Rhodri Morgan AM and the then Minister for Health and Social Services Jane Hutt AM in December 2003. The remit of the group was to assess the progress being made in Wales to safeguard children and young people. The final report of the review group was published in February 2006. The final report expressed concern that:

…the level of commitment to child protection issues varies considerably between sports and most individuals who take on the child protection role are volunteers with many other responsibilities.

('Keeping Us Safe: Report of the Safeguarding Vulnerable Children Review', Rhodri Morgan and Jane Hutt, February 2006, p.64)

In light of this, the review recommended that:

The Sports Council for Wales is to review its present policy regarding child protection and make grant funding to sports organisations conditional upon child protection procedures and routine CRB checks being in place.

('Keeping Us Safe: Report of the Safeguarding Vulnerable Children Review', Rhodri Morgan and Jane Hutt, February 2006, p.73).

The Welsh Assembly Government accepted this recommendation in the response it published in October 2006, stating:

…we recognise that there is scope for strengthening arrangements and will discuss with the Sports Council how this should be achieved.

('Children and Young People: Rights to Action, Welsh Assembly Government's Response to "Keeping Us Safe" – the Report of the Safeguarding Vulnerable Children Review', Welsh Assembly Government, October 2006)

Safeguarding Children: Working Together under the Children Act 2004

'Safeguarding Children: Working Together under the Children Act 2004' is a key guidance document for all organisations providing services for, or working with, children and young people and is the main reference for safeguarding in Wales.

It provides guidance on how agencies should work together to protect children. It covers the roles and responsibilities of all professionals who come into contact with children through their work and describes the child protection process.

This new guidance is due to be published by the Welsh Assembly Government shortly.

Local Safeguarding Children Boards

Since October 2006, each local authority area has developed a Local Safeguarding Children Board (LSCB), which replaced the Area Child Protection Committees (ACPCs). The guidance for the development of LSCBs is contained within 'Safeguarding Children: Working Together under the Children Act 2004'.

Vetting and Barring Scheme

The Safeguarding Vulnerable Groups Act 2006 introduces a new centralised vetting and barring system for England and Wales. While this legislation applies to England and Wales, it is anticipated that the Welsh Assembly Government will be making some regulations relevant to Wales. Currently, it is planned that the scheme will be in operation from some time in 2008.

Information Sharing

Sharing information is vital for early intervention to ensure that children and young people get the services they require. It is also essential to protect children and young people from suffering harm from abuse or neglect and to prevent them from offending. There has been confusion and uncertainty on the part of many professionals and volunteers working with children in all sectors, about when, how and with whom concerns about the welfare or safety of children may be shared with others.

The final chapter of the Welsh Assembly Government's guidance 'Safeguarding Children: Working Together under the Children Act 2004' is dedicated to information sharing, including reference to key principles and the legal background to information sharing.

All Wales Child Protection Procedures

This document contains guidance on roles and responsibilities for reporting concerns about a child's welfare or safety. It is currently being updated in light of the Children Act 2004, but can be downloaded from www.ssiacymru.org.uk/index.cfm?articleid=298

CPSU Guidance: Duty of Care

It is widely accepted that, in relation to children and young people, sports organisations have a duty of care. The purpose of this briefing paper is to clarify what that duty entails and to provide some guidance as to what steps can be taken in order to demonstrate that this duty is being met. In essence, duty of care means that a sports body needs to take such measures as are reasonable in the circumstances to ensure that individuals will be safe in using the activity to which they are invited or to which the activity is *permitted*.

A duty of care may be imposed by common law or statute, by contract, or by acceptance by an individual. In some cases, the law imposes a duty of care (ie the duty of care the police have when they arrest someone).

There is no general duty of care upon members of the public towards the public at large. If, however, there is a formal relationship, for example between a club and a club member or a coach and an athlete, there is a duty of care. When children and young people are involved in organised sports activities and are, to any extent, under the care and/or control of one or more adults, the adult(s) have a duty to take reasonable care to ensure their safety and welfare.

The duty occurs in two ways:

- A **legal** duty of care
- A **moral** duty of care.

The legal duty of care has a strict definition and the most obvious example of this is in health and safety procedures. Clear guidance is provided as to what reasonable steps should be taken to minimise the hazards related to activities, substances or situations.

In many sports activities, given the health and safety considerations, it is recognised that a sports organisation owes a duty of care to its members. However, it is also understood and recognised that accidents can and do happen and that it is not possible to predict every eventuality. Liability for the legal duty of care would only arise when an incident occurs and it can be demonstrated that the risk was foreseeable, but no action had been taken to remedy it. In any subsequent legal action, the courts would apply the following criteria

to determining if an organisation or individual would be held responsible:

- Reasonable forseeability of injury
- Proximity
- Fair, just and reasonable to impose a duty.

The claimant would have to show:

- that they were owed a duty of care
- that the defendant breached this duty
- that they suffered damage as a result of the breach.

It is recognised that there is a higher duty of care owed to children and young people and that this is something that those working with children and young people must recognise. An example of this is the Occupier's Liability Act 1957. This requires that an occupier must be prepared for children to be less careful than adults would be in a similar situation. This will be even more so if the child is known to have learning difficulties or is known to have a medical condition that may make the child more vulnerable than the average to foreseeable risk of harm.

Children and Young People in a Club

Any person in charge of children and young people involved in a sports club has a duty of care and should take all reasonable care for their safety. The duty when involved in a sports club is reasonably straightforward: it is comparable to the duty of a teacher in charge of a class of children of the same age. There have been many cases concerning liability for accidents suffered by school pupils while at school that can be usefully applied to the sports setting. Out of these cases has evolved a general principle, which identifies the expected standard of care for teachers as that of a reasonably prudent parent, taking into account the fact that a teacher will have responsibility for a whole class of children.

This means that teachers are not required to achieve perfection with regard to their supervision of children, but that if they fall below the standards of a reasonably prudent parent and injury is suffered as a result, the teacher may be held to be negligent. Those responsible for the management or supervision of children and young people in a club setting should consider what steps they may need to take in order to demonstrate the reasonable standard of care.

Examples of this could include:

- keeping up-to-date registers of attendance

- keeping up-to-date records of contact details

- maintaining appropriate supervision ratios

- maintaining up-to-date information on specific medical conditions (eg allergies, asthma and epilepsy).

The Management of Health and Safety Regulations 1999 require that employers must make risk assessments and specify controls to reduce the risks of their activities.

Those responsible for sports activities should consider themselves in a similar position to an employer and carry out a risk assessment for their activities. When carrying out risk assessments, it is vital to attend to the requirements relating to the duty of care and the other aspects of health and safety. Some sports have developed risk assessment templates and it is important, if these have been developed, to complete them. It is not necessary to complete an assessment on each individual activity or session if it occurs on a regular basis. An annual or seasonal assessment would be sufficient. However, if hazardous equipment is used as part of the activity, this must be checked before the start of each and every session.

The Moral Duty of Care is more correctly a *responsibility* for safety and welfare. Members of staff have a responsibility for those children and young people, and staff that are under their control.

To determine if a breach of the duty of care has occurred, the ordinary civil law of negligence would be applied. The question is whether the accused in acting, or omitting to act, has failed to reach the standard of a reasonable person. In specialist sports activities, the qualified instructor is responsible for the duty of care of all those taking part, irrespective of their age or position. The key point here is that the individual administering the activity, whatever their status, should be appropriately trained and authorised.

In addition to this, those in charge of children have an additional charge and that is to act in *loco parentis*. This term is best explained as requiring the adult to act as 'a reasonable parent'. You will note that the adult is not necessarily the actual parent but, what the child's parent may permit, the sport may not. So, that while a parent may say that their child can stay out until midnight, a reasonable parent might not.

Within sports organisation, the duty of care would start by ensuring that the activity is authorised and the relevant instructors are qualified for the task, but then would go on to ensure that it is managed in a safe manner throughout.

Reasonable Measures

This is best explained as what is considered to be reasonable. For sport, the CPSU has established the 'Standards for Safeguarding and Protecting Children and Young People in Sport' (2003) to identify what an organisation should reasonably undertake in relation to child protection.

The standards expect sports organisations (governing bodies of sport and county sports partnerships) to have in place policies and procedures to cover:

- a child protection policy (Standard 1)

- procedures and systems (Standard 2)

- prevention (Standard 3)

- codes of practice and behaviour (Standard 4)

- equity (Standard 5)

- communication (Standard 6)

- education and training (Standard 7)

- access to advice and support (Standard 8)

- an implementation plan (Standard 9).

For affiliated clubs, it is reasonable to expect that the governing body or wider organisations' policy and procedures are incorporated into the club constitution and adhered to. For more information on the standards, visit www.thecpsu.org.uk

Other steps that would be considered reasonable measures would include adherence to guidance, advice or directions provided by a sports body or other relevant body. Many sports have developed guidance in relation to travel arrangements, recruitment and selection procedures, as well as training and qualifications, for example. For more information on guidance, please contact the relevant governing body.

This briefing paper, and others, can be found on the Child Protection in Sport Unit website (www.thecpsu.org.uk).

Notes

Notes

Mission Statement

sports coach UK is dedicated to guiding the development and implementation of a coaching system, recognised as a world leader, for all coaches at every level in the UK.

We will work with our partners to achieve this, by promoting:

- professional and ethical values
- inclusive and equitable practice
- agreed national standards of competence as a benchmark at all levels
- a regulated and licensed structure
- recognition, value and appropriate funding and reward
- a culture and structure of innovation, constant renewal and continuous professional development (CPD).